SPARKNOTES

Power Tactics

FOR THE NEW SAT

THE WRITING SECTION
MULTIPLE-CHOICE
QUESTIONS

IDENTIFYING SENTENCE ERRORS
•
IMPROVING SENTENCES
•
IMPROVING PARAGRAPHS

SPARK
NOTES

A DIVISION OF BARNES & NOBLE PUBLISHING

SPARKNOTES is a registered trademark of SparkNotes LLC

Spark Educational Publishing
A Division of Barnes & Noble Publishing
120 Fifth Avenue
New York, NY 10011

ISBN 1-4114-0275-8

Please submit changes or report errors to *www.sparknotes.com/errors*

Printed and bound in Canada.

SAT is the registered trademark of the College Entrance Examination Board, which was not involved in the production of, and does not endorse, this product.

Written by Doug Tarnopol

CONTENTS

INTRODUCTION

Truly effective SAT preparation doesn't need to be painful or time-consuming. SparkNotes' *Power Tactics for the New SAT* is proof that powerful test preparation can be streamlined so that you study only what you need. Instead of toiling away through a 700-page book or an expensive six-week course, you can choose the *Power Tactics* book that gets you where you want to be a lot sooner.

Perhaps you're Kid Math, the fastest number-slinger this side of the Mississippi, but a bit of a bumbler when it comes to words. Or maybe you've got the verbal parts down but can't seem to manage algebraic functions. *Power Tactics for the New SAT* provides an extremely focused review of every component on the new SAT, so you can design your own program of study.

If you're not exactly sure where you fall short, log on to **testprep.sparknotes.com/powertactics** and take our free diagnostic SAT test. This test will pinpoint your weaknesses and reveal exactly where to focus.

Since you're holding this book in your hands, it's pretty likely that the new Writing section's multiple-choice questions are giving you trouble. You've made the right decision because in a few short hours, you will have mastered this part of the exam. No sweat, no major investment of time or money, no problem.

So, let's not waste any time: go forth and conquer the Writing section so you can get on with the *better parts* of your life!

ABOUT
THE NEW SAT

THE OLD

The SAT, first administered in 1926, has undergone a thorough restruc-uring. For the last ten years, the SAT consisted of two sections: Verbal and Math. The Verbal section contained Analogies, Sentence Comple-ions, and Critical Reading passages and questions. The Math section ested arithmetic, algebra, and geometry, as well as some probability, sta-istics, and data interpretation.

You received one point for each correct answer. For most questions, a quarter of a point was deducted for each incorrect answer. This was called the "wrong-answer penalty," which was designed to neutralize random guessing. If you simply filled in the bubble sheet at random, you'd likely get one-fifth of the items correct, given that each item has ive answer choices (excluding student-produced–response items). You'd also get four-fifths of the items wrong, losing $4 \times \frac{1}{4}$, or 1 point for the four incorrectly answered items. Every time you determined an answer choice was wrong, you'd improve your odds by beating the wrong-answer penalty. The net number of points (less wrong-answer penalties) was called the "raw score."

Raw score = # of correct answers – ($\frac{1}{4}$ × # of wrong answers)

That score was then converted to the familiar 200–800 "scaled score."

THE NEW

For 2005, the SAT added a Writing section and an essay, changed the name of *Verbal* to *Critical Reading*, and added algebra II content to the Math section. The following chart compares the old SAT with the new SAT:

Old SAT	New SAT
Verbal	**Critical Reading**
Analogies	*Eliminated*
Sentence Completions	Sentence Completions
Long Reading Passages	Long Reading Passages
Paired Reading Passages	Paired Reading Passages
	Short Reading Passages
Math—Question Types	
Multiple Choice	Multiple Choice
Quantitative Comparisons	*Eliminated*
Student-produced Responses	Student-produced Responses
Math—Content Areas	
Numbers & Operations	Numbers & Operations
Algebra I	Algebra I
	Algebra II
Geometry	Geometry
Data Analysis, Statistics & Probability	Data Analysis, Statistics & Probability
	Writing
	Identifying Sentence Errors
	Improving Sentences
	Improving Paragraphs
	Essay
Total Time: 3 hours	*Total Time*: 3 hours, 45 minutes
Maximum Scaled Score: 1600	*Maximum Scaled Score*: 2400 Separate Essay Score (2–12)

The scoring for the test is the same, except that the Writing section provides a third 200–800 scaled score, and there is now a separate essay score. The wrong-answer penalty is still in effect.

NEW PACKAGE, OLD PRODUCT

While the test has changed for test-*takers*, it has not changed all that much from the test-*maker*'s point of view. The Educational Testing Service (ETS) is a not-for-profit institute that creates the SAT for The College Board. Test creation is not as simple a task as you might think. Any standardized test question has to go through a rigorous series of editorial reviews and statistical studies before it can be released to the public. In fact, that's why the old SAT featured a seventh unscored, "experimental" section: new questions were introduced and tested out in these sections. ETS "feeds" potential questions to its test-takers to measure the level of difficulty. Given the complex and lengthy process of developing new questions, it would be impossible for ETS to introduce *totally* new question types or make major changes to existing question types.

Now that you know these facts, the "new" SAT will start to make more sense. The changes are neither random nor unexpected. Actually, the only truly *new* question type on the SAT is the short reading passage followed by a couple of questions. However, the skills tested and strategies required are virtually identical to the tried-and-true, long reading-passage question type. All other additions to the test consist of new *content* rather than new *question types*. Both multiple-choice and student-produced–response math questions ("grid-ins") now feature algebra II concepts. Same question type, new content. Critical Reading features one fiction passage per test, as well as questions on genre, rhetorical devices, and cause and effect. Same question type, different content.

Even the much-feared new Writing section is in a sense old news. The PSAT and the SAT II Writing tests have featured exactly the same multiple-choice question types for years. The essay format and scoring rubric are virtually identical to those of the SAT II Writing test. The College Board had no other choice, given how long the test-development process is.

The other major changes are omissions, not additions: Quantitative Comparisons and Analogies have been dumped from the test.

So, in a nutshell, ETS has simply attached an SAT II Writing test to the old SAT, dropped Analogies and Quantitative Comparisons, added some algebra II content and short reading passages, and ensured that some fiction and fiction-related questions are included. That's it.

A USER'S GUIDE

Reading this book will maximize your score on the multiple-choice writing section. We've divided up your study into two sections: **Power Tactics** and **Practice Sets**. The Power Tactics will provide you with important concepts and strategies you'll need to tackle multiple-choice writing. The Practice Sets will give you an opportunity to apply what you learn to SAT questions. To achieve your target score, you'll learn:

- The three question types you'll encounter: **Identifying Sentence Errors, Improving Sentences**, and **Improving Paragraphs**.
- What the test-makers are actually trying to test with each multiple-choice writing question type.
- Essential concepts and powerful step methods to maximize your score.
- Test-taking strategies that allow you to approach each section with the best possible mindset.
- The 14 most common mistakes and how to avoid them.

In order to get the most out of this book:

- Make sure to read each section thoroughly and carefully.
- Don't skip the Guided Practice questions.
- Read all explanations to all questions.
- Go to **testprep.sparknotes.com/powertactics** for a free full-length diagnostic **pretest**. This test will help you determine your strengths and weaknesses for multiple-choice writing and for the entire SAT.
- Go back to our website after you complete this book to take a **posttest**. This test will tell you how well you've mastered multiple-choice writing and what topics you still need to review.

STUDYING FOR IMPROVING PARAGRAPHS

There are far fewer Improving Paragraph questions per test than the other two question types. Therefore, *preparing* for Improving Paragraphs, which requires more complex and higher-order skills than the sentence questions, is a *higher* investment of your study time for a *lower* yield of points. Dealing with Paragraph Improvements requires you to tackle both a *passage* and related *questions*.

Unless you're already scoring fairly high[*] on the Writing section, or you have a lot of time before the actual test, concentrate on Identifying Sentence Errors and Improving Sentences. Since the latter questions greatly outnumber the Improving Paragraph questions, you'll only "need" the Improving Paragraph points if you're already scoring fairly high.

If you determine that you should concentrate on Identifying Sentence Errors and Improving Sentences, skip all the Improving Paragraph sections and practice sets in this book, including "Clear and Concise Writing" in the Essential Concepts section.

---

[*] "Fairly high" would be well above the average score, which is 500 on the 200–800 scale. As a rule of thumb, if your SAT score is not within shouting distance of 600, concentrate on the sentence-level question types.

THE POWER TACTICS

ANATOMY OF MULTIPLE-CHOICE WRITING

Before plunging into the deep end of the pool, we need to wade through some basics, including the fundamental structure of the SAT question type itself. That's why we provide you with an X-ray of the multiple-choice writing question. By looking at these questions inside and out, you'll know more about how The College Board tests your skills and how to approach each and every question you'll encounter on the SAT.

The new SAT Writing section consists of three types of multiple-choice questions and one essay. This book is concerned with the multiple-choice questions; the essay is treated in a separate book in this series.

The three types of multiple-choice questions are, officially:

- Identifying Sentence Errors
- Improving Sentences
- Improving Paragraphs

Since these official names are kind of clunky, we'll refer to these question types, respectively, as:

- Sentence Error ID
- Sentence Improvement
- Paragraph Improvement

Let's take a look at an example of each question type and the terms we'll use to refer to their various parts.

SENTENCE ERROR ID

1. <u>In Victorian</u> England, hunger and unemployment <u>was</u> so prevalent
    AB

    that social revolution was a constant source of <u>anxiety for</u> members
    C

    of the <u>upper class.</u> <u>No error</u>
    D E

The entire sentence is the **item**. The lettered, underlined portions of the sentence are the **answer choices**. One of these five answer choices is correct. The others are called **distractors**, because they are designed to *distract* attention away from the correct answer choice. (Don't worry about the answer right now; you'll see this item again.)

Note that choice **E** means that the item has no error. Since there are five answer choices, expect roughly 20 percent of Sentence Error IDs to have no errors.

SENTENCE IMPROVEMENT

1. Eager to pass his final exams, <u>studying was the student's top priority</u>.

(A)   studying was the student's top priority.
(B)   the student made studying his top priority.
(C)   the top priority of the student was studying.
(D)   the student's top priority was studying.
(E)   studying was the top priority for the student.

The sentence containing the underlined portion is the **stem**. The lettered options beneath the stem are the answer choices. Four of these are the incorrect distractors; one is correct. (Again, don't worry about the answer right now. You'll get another crack at this item later on.) The item consists of both the stem *and* answer choices.

Note that choice **A** reproduces the underlined portion of the stem. This is always the case. Choice **A** is essentially Sentence Improvement's "No error" choice. Expect roughly 20 percent of Sentence Improvements to need no improvement.

PARAGRAPH IMPROVEMENT

(1) Japanese cuisine continues to grow in popularity in the United States. (2) Americans are already fond of Chinese food. (3) Now they are discovering that Japanese cuisine takes a similar set of basic ingredients and transforms them into something quite special. (4) That Japanese food is generally low in fat and calories, and offers many options for vegetarians and vegans, adds to its popularity.

(5) Americans' enjoyment of Japanese cooking is still largely limited to an occasional night out at a Japanese restaurant. (6) Actually, Japanese cooking is surprisingly simple. (7) Anyone with a standard set of cooking utensils and knowledge of basic cooking terms can easily follow the recipes in any Japanese cookbook

(8) Since Japanese restaurants tend to be fairly expensive, one would think that fans of the cuisine would be excited about the possibility of making it at home. (9) Unfortunately, many traditional Japanese recipes call for costly ingredients that often can only be found at Asian grocery stores. (10) As these ingredients become more widely available at lower prices, we are sure to see a proportional increase in the number of people cooking Japanese food at home.

1. In context, what is the best way to revise and combine sentences 2 and 3 (reproduced below)?

   Americans are already fond of Chinese food. Now they are discovering that Japanese cuisine takes a similar set of basic ingredients and transforms them into something quite special.

(A) American people are already fond of Chinese food, and have discovered that Japanese cuisine takes a similar set of basic ingredients and transforms them into something quite special.

(B) American people are already fond of Chinese food, and now discover that Japanese cuisine takes a similar set of basic ingredients and transforms them into something quite special.

(C) Already fond of Chinese food, American people are now discovering that Japanese cuisine takes a similar set of basic ingredients and transforms them into something quite special.

(D) Already fond of Chinese food, having discovered that Japanese cuisine takes a similar set of basic ingredients and transforms them into something quite special, American people like it.

(E) American people are already fond of Chinese food; however, they are discovering that Japanese cuisine takes a similar set of basic ingredients and transforms them into something quite special.

2. In context, what is the best word to add to the beginning of sentence 5?

(A) Yet,
(B) Moreover,
(C) Predictably,
(D) Fortunately,
(E) Undoubtedly,

3. What would be the best phrase to add to the end of sentence 5 to improve the transition to sentence 6?

(A) , because people do not like to eat ethnic food on a regular basis.

(B) , and this has led to many restaurant closings.

(C) , and for far too long it has been assumed that this food is difficult to make in one's own kitchen.

(D) , because the recent economic recession has forced people to reduce their spending.

(E) , and this means that Japanese cuisine may disappear from America entirely.

4. What would be the best subject for a sentence inserted after sentence 7?

(A) The rising popularity of other ethnic cuisine
(B) An example of a simple Japanese recipe
(C) A summary of the points made so far
(D) Data on the profitability of Japanese restaurants
(E) Information on where to buy Japanese cooking utensils

5. Which phrase best describes the purpose of the passage?

(A) To encourage people to eat at Japanese restaurants more often
(B) To record America's increasing interest in ethnic food
(C) To predict a future increase in Japanese cooking in American homes
(D) To discourage people from eating unhealthy food
(E) To promote the purchase of expensive cooking equipment

We refer to the paragraphs on page 14 as the **passage**. Every sentence in the passage is numbered.

As with Sentence Error ID and Sentence Improvement, an item consists of a stem and five answer choices. The Paragraph Improvement stems sometimes include an excerpt taken directly from the passage, as in the first item. Part of this excerpt is often underlined in order to direct your attention to the particular portion of the excerpt. Four of the answer choices are distractors; one is correct.

The entire unit of passage-plus-items is called a **set**. We also use *set* to refer to all the Sentence Error ID items or all the Sentence Improvement items in a given Writing section. (We return to this particular set later in the book, so stay tuned for answers and explanations.)

WHAT MULTIPLE-CHOICE WRITING ACTUALLY TESTS

The Writing section tests your ability to *recognize* and *correct* poorly written sentences, paragraphs, and passages. The Writing section does *not* test your knowledge of grammatical terminology. However, it *does* test your ability to recognize and fix incorrect use of grammar. In addition, the Writing section tests certain features of good writing such as the proper use of particular **idiomatic expressions** and **voice**. (Don't worry if you're not familiar with these terms—you will be by the end of this book.) In other words, the Writing section tests not only grammar but also style and word choice.

While anything tested in Sentence Error ID and Sentence Improvement is fair game in Paragraph Improvement, Paragraph Improvement also tests features of good writing beyond proper sentence construction. Paragraph Improvement primarily tests your ability to make an essay clearer and more concise.

The good news is that the Writing section tests a limited number of grammatical and stylistic concepts. How can we be so sure given that the Writing section is brand-new? These Writing section items have been part of the PSAT and SAT II Writing for a long time. Additionally, The College Board has never made a secret of exactly what skills these items (or any SAT items) test.

If you understand what the SAT likes to test, you'll have a much better chance of recognizing the errors. The SAT Writing section will test the following broad concepts:

- Verb Tense
- Subject/Verb Agreement
- Noun/Number Agreement
- Pronoun/Number Agreement
- Pronoun Case
- Ambiguous and Vague Pronouns
- Modifiers and Modification
- Clause Organization
- Comparisons and Parallelism
- Idioms and Word Choice
- Active Voice and Passive Voice
- Clear and Concise Writing

Don't worry if you don't recognize some (or any) of these terms. That's why you're reading this book!

ESSENTIAL CONCEPTS

Although the Writing section requires you to master some discrete concepts, what follows is not meant to be an exhaustive lesson in grammar. We've pared that huge subject down to what actually matters for the new SAT Writing section. As you study these concepts, don't get too caught up in the formal names. The names are there simply because we have to call these concepts something. Concentrate on the concepts *behind* the names.

Keep in mind that half your battle will simply be recognizing when something is wrong in a Writing section item. For a Sentence Error ID, that's the whole battle. If you recognize that something isn't quite right in a Sentence Improvement or Paragraph Improvement, you'll be most of the way toward being able to predict and recognize the fix among the answer choices.

Once you're familiar with these concepts, we'll practice applying your knowledge to SAT items by following our specific step methods.

VERB TENSE

Verbs are the motor of language—literally, they're where the action is. Anyone who has struggled with a foreign language knows that verb tenses can get *really* complicated. Luckily the vast majority of Writing items tests only a handful of key concepts. They center on knowing the proper **form** each tense of the verb takes (known as "inflection").

Past vs. Present Perfect

The **past tense** signifies that something has occurred or existed in the past. It is indicated by an *-ed* inflection or an equivalent irregular form, such as *swam* or *sank*.

Helen **lived** in Troy long ago.

This means that Helen lived in Troy at some *definite* point in the past. She no longer lives there, for whatever reason.

The **present perfect tense** refers either to something that began in the past and continues into the present or something that occurred in the past but still has some bearing on the present. It is indicated by using *has/have* plus the *-ed* (or the equivalent irregular) form of a verb:

Helen **has lived** in Troy before.

Unlike the previous sentence, this sentence means that Helen lived in Troy at some *unspecified* point in the past.

Helen **has lived** in Troy for twenty years.

This sentence means that Helen started living in Troy at some point in the past, never left, and is still living there in the present.

There are a few words that signal that the present perfect rather than the past should be used. These **signpost words** are:

Signpost Word	Example	Comment
ever	*Helen has loved Paris ever since she laid eyes on him.*	Notice how this sentence uses both the present perfect and the past. *Helen has loved Paris* means that Helen started loving Paris at some point in the past and still loves him in the present. *[E]ver since she laid eyes on him* means that all that lovin' started at a definite point in the past—when she first saw Paris.

Signpost Word	Example	Comment
never	*Helen has never been one to restrain herself.*	This means that at no point in the past—and up to the present moment—has Helen been able to control herself. A state of being that began at some indefinite point in the past has continued up to the present moment.
since	*There has been constant war since Helen came to Troy.*	Again, an action has occurred at some indefinite point in the past and continues to this day.
yet	*She hasn't fled to Troy yet.*	A particular state of being—that of not fleeing to Troy—has not occurred since some indefinite point in the past and continues not to occur up to the present moment.

Past vs. Past Perfect

The **past perfect tense** (also known as "pluperfect") refers to something that began and ended *before* something else occurred in the past. The past perfect tense is "more past than the past." It is indicated by using *had* plus the *-ed* (or equivalent irregular) form:

Helen **had lived** in Sparta before she lived in Troy.

This means that Helen's presence in Sparta *preceded* her presence in Troy, which *itself* occurred in the past.

As a rule, if there are two actions that occurred in the past, put the one that occurred deeper in the past in the past perfect tense. The more recent action should be in the past tense.

If-clauses

What's the difference between the following two sentences?

If I see another reference to *The Iliad*, I will scream.
If I were Helen, I would not leave Sparta.

he first sentence states that if a condition is fulfilled (seeing another *Iliad* reference), then a particular action will result (a scream). The second sentence states something that's contrary to fact, something imagined that exists only in thought. The person making that statement is *not* Helen, clearly, but is projecting himself into that person's situation.

The first sentence is in the **indicative** mood; the second sentence is in the **subjunctive** mood. (Again, don't worry too much about the names used here.)

The main point for SAT Writing is the form of the second (subjunctive) sentence. The *if*-clause should never include a *would*-verb; *would* is used only in the second clause, which we'll call the *would*-clause:

Incorrect	Correct	Comment on Correct Version
If you would have come earlier, you would have seen him.	If you had come earlier, you would have seen him.	*If*-clause is in past perfect. *Would*-clause is in present perfect.

SUBJECT/VERB AGREEMENT

Trojans is doomed.
Hector are violent.

It's easy to see what's wrong with these sentences: the subjects (*Trojans* and *Hector*) do not match their verbs (*is* and *are*, respectively). *Trojans* are plural but *is* is singular; *Hector* is singular, but *are* is plural. Subjects and verbs must match or "agree."

The SAT will test this by sticking a long phrase or clause between the subject and the verb, like so:

The importation of predator species, which stems from a laudable desire to break with the usual chemical methods of pest control, almost always lead to ecological imbalance.

See the error? If not, get rid of the intervening clause:

The importation of predator species almost always lead to ecological imbalance.

Can you see it now? If you still can't see it, isolate the subject and verb:

The importation of predator species almost always lead to
　　　　　　Subject　　　　　　　　　　　　　　　Verb
ecological imbalance.

Predator species is not the subject—*the **importation** of predator species is.*
Importation is singular; *lead* is the plural form of the verb. The singular
form of the verb must match the singular subject.

Hector **leads** the Trojans.
The Trojans **lead** all Anatolian city-states.

The correct version is as follows:

The importation of predator species, which stems from a laudable
desire to break with the usual chemical methods of pest control,
almost always leads to ecological imbalance.

Is the following sentence correct?

Inside the wooden horse is Achilles and Odysseus.

Tricky! The subject is hidden here—it's **not** *the wooden horse.* What if you
flipped the sentence around so the subject, which we're accustomed to
seeing at the beginning of a sentence, comes first:

Achilles and Odysseus is inside the wooden horse.

The *is* sticks out more when the sentence is rewritten this way; it should
be *are. Achilles and Odysseus* is a compound subject; compound subjects
take plural verbs. Only the word *and* can create a compound subject. *As
well as*, *or*, and *along with* do **not** create compound subjects.

Bill and Ted **are** excellent adventurers.
Bill, as well as Ted, **is** an excellent adventurer.
Bill, along with Ted, **is** an excellent adventurer.
Bill or Ted **is** an excellent adventurer.

What, if anything, is wrong with the following sentence?

Neither of those two airhead adventurers are bright.

The problem is that *neither*, *either*, and *none* take singular, not plural, verbs. The correction is:

Neither of those two airhead adventurers is bright.

Finally, watch out for nouns that seem plural but are actually singular, such as:

The **series** of lectures <u>was</u> very interesting.
The **team** <u>was</u> ready for the big game.
The **couple** <u>finds</u> happiness in each other.

Series, *team*, and *couple* are singular nouns that refer to groups. *Group*, actually, is another good example. By definition, a group has more than one member, but a group itself is singular: one group; many groups.

NOUN/NUMBER AGREEMENT

All birds are very good at building their nest.

This may look OK, but it's incorrect. As written, it means that all birds currently alive, as well as all birds that have ever lived, are very good at building the **one nest** they've all shared. That's a big nest!

Nouns have to agree in number—start with plural, end with plural; start with singular, end with singular. This sentence should be:

All **birds** are very good at building their **nests**.

Here's another common mistake that the SAT will likely throw at you:

Donna and Doug are planning to sell all their possessions and move to Maui in order to become a beach bum.

How can **two** people, *Donna and Doug*, become **one** beach bum? Well, they can't:

Donna and Doug are planning to sell all their possessions and move to Maui in order to become **beach bums**.

Another commonly tested feature of nouns is **countability**. Look at the following sentences:

I have many failings.
To mature is to transcend much failure.

Both sentences are correct. *Failings* is something one could count; *failings* are discrete entities like pebbles or atoms or four-leaf clovers. *Failure*, however, cannot be counted; *failure* is an abstract state of being, like *sorrow*, *liberty*, and *happiness*. "I'll take two happinesses please, just in case I break one"—if only! Concrete entities can be **noncountable** as well: *air* and *water*, to name two. (*Putting on airs* and *parting the waters* are figuratively countable uses of these noncountable nouns.)

Countability is most often tested via the *less/fewer* and *number/amount* pairings. Here's a handy chart:

Noun	Count-able?	Use	Example
hatred	no	less	You would be wise to show less hatred toward others.
pony	yes	fewer	There are fewer ponies romping here than I had hoped.
love	no	less	The less love you provide, the less you'll receive.
kiss	yes	fewer	I would suffer if you bestowed fewer kisses on me.
mango	yes	number	I ate a large number of mangoes right off the tree when I was in Maui.
money	no	amount	The amount of money I spent in Maui is less that you might think.
shark	yes	number	There are a number of sharks off Maui's coast.
fear	no	amount	The amount of fear these sharks cause is way out of proportion to the actual danger they represent.

PRONOUN/NUMBER AGREEMENT

Did everyone remember to bring their permission slip with them?

The question above is grammatically incorrect.

Everyone is singular, strange as that may seem, and refers to a collection of people. It also refers to each individual in a collection of people—every*one*.

To highlight this error, substitute the equivalent phrase *each of you* into the *permission slip* sentence:

Did each of you remember to bring their permission slip with them?

The pronoun *their* is plural, but it refers back to a singular subject, *each of you*—or, in the previous sentence, *everyone*. The proper form is:

Did everyone remember to bring **his or her** permission slip with **him or her**?

Yes, this is cumbersome, but correct.

The following words behave just like *everyone*: *anyone*, *no one*, *nobody*, *every*, and *each*.

On another topic, check out this sentence:

Acme Widgets reported today that their earnings had fallen sharply.

Widgets may be plural, but presumably there is only one company called *Acme Widgets*. If it's a single company, it requires a singular pronoun:

Acme Widgets reported today that **its** earnings had fallen sharply.

Anytime you see a plural pronoun in a Writing item, check the noun or pronoun it refers to and replaces (its **antecedent**) to see whether this *very* common error is being tested.

Watch out for "pronoun shift" too:

Incorrect: If *you* start with a particular pronoun, *one* shouldn't shift to another later on in the sentence.

Correct: So, if *one* would like to do as well as *one* can on the SAT, keep this commonly tested error in mind.

Correct: That way, *you* will be happy with the score *you* receive.

PRONOUN CASE

If you've ever struggled with German, Latin, or Russian, you know how nasty **case** can be. Case inflections display the relationship between a noun or pronoun and other words in a sentence. Case in nouns and pronouns is a little bit like tense in verbs, because both case and tense can cause words to change form. English has cases, too, but thanks to the "Frenchification" of English, the language has lost many of its Germanic case inflections.

But not all. Pronouns can get *quite* complicated—there are six classes of pronouns—so let's keep things simple and SAT-related:

Singular Personal Pronouns

Person	Subjective Case	Objective Case	Possessive Case
First	I	me	my, mine
Second	you	you	your, yours
Third	he, she, it	him, her, it	his, her, hers, its

Plural Personal Pronouns

Person	Subjective Case	Objective Case	Possessive Case
First	we	us	our, ours
Second	you	you	your, yours
Third	they	them	their, theirs

The subjective case is used when a pronoun is the subject of a sentence:

I loved Helen.

The **subject** of this sentence, or the person who is performing or acting the verb *loved*, is *I*; the **object** of *I*'s affection is *Helen*.

The objective case is used when a pronoun is the object of a sentence:

Helen loved **me**.

The **possessive** case is used to show ownership (i.e., possession), regardless of where it appears in the sentence:

Possessive subject: **My** face launched a thousand ships.
Possessive object: He looked into **my** eyes.

So far, so good. However, things can get dicey when the sentences get more complex:

My husband is searching for Paris and I.
You and me need to get out of Sparta as quickly as possible.
Quick, Helen, grab me sword!

Each sentence is incorrect. How can you tell? Always ask yourself: "What's the subject? What's the object? What shows possession?"
In the first sentence, *My husband* is the subject and *Paris and I* is the object. So use the objective case for the first person pronoun, not the subjective case:

My husband is searching for Paris and **me**.

In the second sentence, *You and me* is the subject, so you need to use the subjective case for the first person pronoun, not the objective case:

You and **I** need to get out of Sparta as quickly as possible.

In the third sentence, the *sword* belongs to the person asking Helen to grab it for him. Possession equals possessive case:

Quick, Helen, grab **my** sword!

Another frequently tested feature of pronoun case—one that usually makes students' heads explode—is the infamous *who* vs. *whom*. There is no consensus among authorities on how to use *who* and *whom*. However, *our* only authority is spelled S-A-T, which has taken a fairly conservative stance on this controversial issue:

Who is subjective; *whom* is objective.
(*Whose*, by the way, is the possessive form.)

So:

The woman **who** stole my heart keeps it still.

This is correct. *Who* refers back to *the woman*, who is the subject; there-fore, the subjective case is used.

The woman **whom** I could not keep from stealing my heart keeps it still.

This sentence is also correct, at least in SAT-land. *Whom* refers not to the subject, *the woman*, but to the object, *I could not keep from stealing my heart*. The following examples bring out this subtle difference:

If the question is . . .	then the answer is . . .	because . . .
Who causes the destruction of Troy?	**Helen** is the woman **who** causes the destruction of Troy.	The focus is on the identity of the woman (*Helen*), which is the subject of this sentence. So, use *who*.
We see the destruction of Troy caused by **whom**?	Helen is the woman **whom** we see cause the destruction of Troy.	The focus is on what *we*, the audience, see. *We* are the object, so use *whom*.

Generally you should use *whom* after a preposition:

The woman **to whom** I gave my heart keeps it still.

Don't fret too much over this, as the need for *who* or *whom* is made pretty clear in a given item.

AMBIGUOUS AND VAGUE PRONOUNS

Starting to hate pronouns? Don't worry, this concept is much more intui-tive than the last one.

Ambiguous pronouns lack a clear antecedent, while vague pronouns lack an antecedent altogether. Remember that antecedent refers to the noun or pronoun that a pronoun refers to (*ante* meaning "before" in Latin).

In the following sentence, the pronoun is bolded:

Fred visited Bob after **his** graduation.

Let's play "Find the Antecedent." Whose graduation are we talking about? Fred's or Bob's? They're both men, so it's impossible to tell. This kind of mistake can slide right by a careful test-taker, so be on the lookout. Replace *his* with either *Fred's* or *Bob's,* and you've solved the problem:

Fred visited Bob after **Fred's** graduation.

Or:

Fred visited Bob after **Bob's** graduation.

Do not assume that logic trumps grammar on the SAT. Look at the following sentence:

Zelda gave her daughter a bike that she rode constantly from that moment on.

This seems less ambiguous because we tend to interpret the sentence according to our experience and expectations: mother gives daughter a bicycle; daughter is totally psyched; daughter thus rides bike nonstop. *She* refers to *her daughter*; choose **E**, No error, and keep going.

That's all well and good, except that you just chose a distractor! It is possible that Zelda gave her daughter a bike and that Zelda, not her daughter, rode that bike constantly from that moment on. Maybe Zelda's a mean mom. Maybe the daughter hated the bicycle and Zelda rekindled her childhood love of cycling. The point is, we've got an ambiguous pronoun, and that's an error.[*]

---

[*] Many people are taught that since *her daughter* is closest to *she*, *her daughter* is *she*'s antecedent. Word order helps determine antecedent. But the SAT has its own take on this, and that's all that matters for our purposes.

Now, what's wrong with the following sentence?

They say that the SAT considers vague pronouns to be a grammatical mistake.

On its own, the *they* in this sentence has no antecedent at all. There are many ways to rewrite this sentence, but here's one option:

The author of this book says that the SAT considers vague pronouns to be a grammatical mistake.

Now you have a clear statement. Note, however, that if the original sentence had been embedded in a paragraph, it would be clear who *They* refers to:

I've talked to three English teachers. They say that the SAT considers vague pronouns to be a grammatical mistake. I'm glad I asked them about it.

Context is everything. In this context, *They* has a clear antecedent: *three English teachers.*

MODIFIERS AND MODIFICATION

A **modifier** is a word or a phrase that describes another word or phrase. The most familiar examples are **adjectives** and **adverbs**. Adjectives describe nouns or pronouns. Adverbs describe verbs, adjectives, or other adverbs. (Articles—*the, a, an*—are also considered adjectives by some authorities.)

Here are some examples:

Adjectives
The **dark** night hid all.
The **harmful** rays of the sun penetrated the skin.

Adverbs
Laurie ran **quickly**.
Ziki spoke French **fluently**.

The SAT often tests whether an adjective or an adverb is required. For example, why is the following sentence incorrect?

My dog smelled terrible before his bath.

Terrible is an adjective modifying *smelled*, which is a verb. That's a no-no; it should be:

My dog smelled terribly before his bath.

In addition to testing whether a sentence needs an adverb or an adjective, the SAT will very likely test whether you use the proper form of an adjective. Adjectives can take three forms:

Descriptive	Comparative	Superlative
sharp	sharper	sharpest
cold	colder	coldest
fascinating	more fascinating	most fascinating
good	better	best
bad	worse	worst

Most adjectives follow the regular forms exemplified by *sharp* and *cold*. Some, like *fascinating*, require *more* for the comparative and *most* for the superlative. *Good* and *bad*, and some others, are irregular.

Consider the following sentences:

Of the three knives, that one is sharper.
That knife is sharpest than this one.

Both are incorrect. The comparative form should be used with two objects; the superlative with three or more objects. The sentences should be:

Of the three knives, that one is **sharpest**.
That knife is **sharper** than this one.

Phrases can act as modifiers, too, and this is where things get a little trickier:

Racing down the country road, Carlos felt rejuvenated by the crisp morning air.

The phrase *racing down the country road* is a unit that modifies *Carlos*. But what if we wrote the sentence another way?

Racing down the country road, the crisp morning air rejuvenated Carlos.

What this second sentence is saying is that *the crisp morning air* was *racing down the country road* as it *rejuvenated Carlos.* This is the storied **dangling modifier**. The modifier *racing down the country road* dangles off the front of the sentence, unconnected to *Carlos*, the word it modifies. You will likely see a bunch of these on the test—the SAT *loves* to test this concept. Some other examples of dangling modifiers follow; they can be pretty funny once you recognize the error:

Incorrect: Smoking a big cigar, the baby was admired by its father.
Comment: There's very little chance that any baby would be precocious enough to smoke a cigar.
Correct: Smoking a big cigar, the father admired his baby.

Incorrect: Sweating profusely from the exertion, there are some drawbacks to cycling in the summer.
Comment: This modifier is dangling by a thread—what could *sweating profusely from the exertion* modify in this sentence?
Correct: One of the drawbacks of summer cycling is that you'll sweat profusely.

Incorrect: Sweating profusely from the exertion, my shirt was soaked in five minutes.
Comment: Was *the shirt* doing the *sweating*? I think not!
Correct: Sweating profusely from the exertion, I soaked my shirt in five minutes.

Incorrect: To stave off dehydration, a lot of water should be drunk while biking.

Comment: We're missing the noun that needs modification—*who* needs to stave off dehydration?

Correct: To stave off dehydration, bikers should drink a lot of water.

Here's an example of another error that shows up a lot on the SAT: the **misplaced modifier**. Typically, adverbs are to blame for this very common mistake:

He nearly hit that ball out of the park.

What's wrong with that, you ask? The golden rule of modification, as you may have guessed, is: **Keep the modifier as close to what it modifies as possible.** That's exactly what the author of this sentence did: *nearly* modifies the verb *hit*. OK, so what's the problem? Well, sometimes this rule is broken for the sake of clarity and logic. What, exactly, does it mean to *nearly hit* something? Isn't that kind of like *missing* it? That's not what happened, clearly, so fix the sentence like so:

He hit that ball nearly out of the park.

Now what happened is crystal clear: the batter hit the ball and almost knocked it out of the park.

CLAUSE ORGANIZATION

A **clause** is a group of words that has a subject and a predicate. Sentences can have one clause or many clauses. You won't often see a sentence with more than three clauses in the SAT Writing section. You will see a good number of SAT items that test clause organization.

The following sentence has three clauses, each of which is underlined:

<u>Bob Dylan stunned many of his fans</u> when
Clause 1
<u>he appeared in a lingerie commercial in 2004</u> because
Clause 2
<u>much of his career had been devoted to debunking empty commercialism.</u>
Clause 3

The words that are not underlined are the all-important connections between the clauses. They guide the reader from clause to clause, and the SAT will test your ability to choose these words appropriately. Appropriate connections—technically known as **conjunctions** and **connectives**—require that you follow logic, as well as grammar.

In the sentence above, *when* lets the reader know that the trigger for Dylan's fans' surprise is coming. Since *when* is a temporal word, it indicates that something specific happened at some specific point in time, and you're about to be told what that was. *Because* indicates that the reason why some of his fans were so stunned is about to be revealed.

English has many such guide words and phrases. Individual SAT tests will not include them all, but here's a handy list of some common ones:

also	consequently	nevertheless	still
although	despite	no less than	therfore
and	even	or	though
as well as	for	otherwise	thus
because	however	since	yet
but	moreover	so	

The Weak *And*

One commonly tested feature of clause organization could be called "the weak *and*." *And* is pretty much the word-version of the + symbol and denotes addition or the mere presence of two equivalent things at the same time or in the same place:

Bill likes ketchup and John likes mustard.

"Big deal," you say, but the *and* here doesn't serve as much of a guide word. The SAT tests whether you can recognize this type of weak *and*. Look at this sentence:

Bob Dylan's appearance in a lingerie commercial stunned many of his fans and much of his career had been devoted to debunking empty commercialism.

Huh? This sentence just cries out for causation. Substitute *because* for *and* to make this sentence be all that it can be:

Bob Dylan's appearance in a lingerie commercial stunned many of his fans **because** much of his career had been devoted to debunking empty commercialism.

Commas, Semicolons, and Colons

A related and much-tested concept concerns **commas**, **semicolons**, and **colons**. These punctuation marks act as connection-words: they are short-hand for certain types of connections between clauses.

If a period is a "full stop," and a comma is a "pause," then a semicolon is somewhere in between, but closer to a full stop. Use it to separate two clauses that could stand alone as sentences:

> To err is human; some of us are more human than others are.
> To err is human. Some of us are more human than others are.

Use a colon either to "announce" a list or to magnify or exemplify what preceded the colon:

> You forgot to pack three key items: a flashlight, a first aid kit, and a pair of sunglasses.

> Most of the troublemakers in my class are actually gifted students: Kim, for example, consistently receives high scores on aptitude tests.

Like semicolons, colons can separate clauses that can stand alone. However, a colon stresses that the clause after the colon follows sequentially from the phrase that precedes the colon:

> To err is human; some of us are more human than others are.
> To err is human: some of us are more human than others are.

The first sentence indicates that all people make mistakes, but, as an almost statistical point, some of us tend to make more mistakes than others do. The second sentence places more emphasis on the fact that certain people make more mistakes than most do.

That vs. Which

Commas are the hardest of all punctuation marks to master. Luckily the SAT tests a few key mistakes, such as the Montagues and the Capulets of the pronoun world, *that* and *which*. Read the following two sentences:

> The car that I had repaired is in the driveway.
> The car, which I had to have repaired, is in the driveway.

The first sentence tells you which car is in the driveway: *that I had repaired* is a modifier of *the car*. It performs the same function that "red" or "blue" would if either was substituted for *that I had repaired*. It's a response to the question, Where did you park the car you had repaired? The second sentence reports the repair of the car as incidental. *Which* is used, and the *which*-clause is set off with commas. It's a response to the question, Where is the car? If you see a *which*-clause, make sure that commas set it off. Often the SAT will omit one of the commas.

Comma Splice

Another commonly tested error is the **comma splice**. Don't use a comma where a period or semicolon is required:

> To err is human, some of us are more human than others are.

This is a comma splice, pal, which is a type of **fused sentence,** also known as a **run-on sentence**. Fix them with a semicolon or period. The SAT *loves* this concept!

Sentence Fragments

Watch out for sentence fragments too. A **fragment** occurs when a poor, insecure, dependent clause that cannot stand on its own is forced to do so. These clauses often contain **gerunds** (*-ing* constructions) or **infinitives**:

> Swelling to twice its size.
> To reach your target score on the SAT.

Fragments make you want to grab that poor lonely clause by the collar and yell, "Where's the payoff? Don't leave me hanging!" Resist the temptation. Understand that a happy sentence needs both a subject and a predicate. Dependent clauses need a more self-sufficient clause for support. Fragments show up quite a bit in Paragraph Improvement.

COMPARISONS AND PARALLELISM

What's wrong with the following sentence?

> Like birds, wings have evolved in some mammals.

What's being compared here? *Birds* and *wings* or *birds* and *some mammals*? Right, *birds* and *some mammals*. To fix this, put the two things being compared next to each other:

Like birds, some mammals have evolved wings.

Another, trickier example:

Like the Byzantines, Ottoman buildings often feature huge domes.

It's illogical to compare *the Byzantines* to *Ottoman buildings*. You're comparing people to structures. Instead, compare like with like. Here are some ways to fix this problem:

Like <u>Byzantine structures</u>, <u>Ottoman buildings</u> often feature huge domes.

Like <u>the Byzantines</u>, <u>the Ottomans</u> built structures that feature huge domes.

Like <u>Byzantine architects</u>, <u>Ottoman architects</u> built structures with huge domes.

Watch out for that typical SAT distraction, the long intervening clause:

Like the Byzantines, who in the course of ruling the eastern Mediterranean basin for a thousand years left behind much-imitated traditions in law, art, and architecture, Ottoman architecture often features huge domes.

No matter how long that intervening clause is, you still have to compare like with like; this sentence compares *the Byzantines* with *Ottoman architecture.* Note how the word *architecture* comes right before *Ottoman architecture*. This is a typical SAT device intended to camouflage the mistake. There are many possible fixes: either compare Byzantines to Ottomans, Byzantine architecture to Ottoman architecture, Byzantine buildings to Ottoman buildings, Byzantine architects to Ottoman architects . . . you get the idea. This kind of error comes up a lot in Sentence and Paragraph Improvements.

Another key concept is the difference between *like* and *as*. Use *like* to compare **nouns** (persons, places, things, or ideas):

> **That woman** sings like **Aretha Franklin**.
> **This desert** looks like **the surface of the moon**.
> **That piece of chicken** you cooked for me is like **iron.**
> **Neoconservatism** sounds an awful lot like **Wilsonianism** to me.

Use *as* to compare **verbs**:

> That woman **sings** powerfully, just as Aretha Franklin **did**.
> This desert **looks** barren, just as the surface of the moon **does**.
> Neoconservatism **sounds** like a bad idea to me, just as Wilsonianism **did** to observers in the 1910s.

For the *like* version of the chicken sentence above, compare the actions rather than the things and use *as*:

> That piece of chicken you cooked for me is hard, just as iron is.

A bit inelegant, isn't it? The following is better:

> That piece of chicken you cooked for me is as hard as iron.

As/as is one of a few important constructions used for comparison. Others are:

Form	Example
neither/nor	That candidate has neither the experience nor the stomach to run for national office.
either/or	Some maintain that a leader can be either honest or effective.
not only/but also	Others maintain that if we simply change the political culture, we can have leaders that are not only honest but also effective.
the more/the more	The more things change, the more they stay the same.
the less/the less	The less people care, the less chance there is anything will change.

Form	Example
both/and	Both liberals and conservatives hunger for more effective government.
if/then	If a candidate appeals to what's best in all citizens, then that candidate will win in a landslide.

These forms should always be maintained: Don't write *neither/or* or *not only/but*. Also, notice how the underlined portions in the example sentences all follow the same form. In other words, these forms are "parallel." Look at this sentence:

I eat lots of vegetables, but on the other hand, I eat lots of fish.

You have the *other hand*, but where's the first hand? This sentence is not parallel; to fix it, write:

On the one hand, I eat lots of vegetables, but on the other hand, I eat lots of fish.

What's wrong with the following sentence?

Not only do I like to ski, but I also like sledding

The verb in the first clause is an infinitive: *to ski*. But the verb in the second clause is a gerund: *sledding.* Fix it in one of two ways:

Not only do I like to ski, but I also like to sled.
Not only do I like skiing, but I also like sledding.

The need for parallel structure arises in series as well. The following sentence is incorrect:

Achilles liked killing, running, and to sulk.

Again, there are two ways to fix this:

Achilles liked to kill, to run, and to sulk.
Achilles liked killing, running, and sulking.

Another version of the parallelism mistake you're likely to see is:

Painting with oils is easier than when you paint with watercolors.

To fix this, make sure your verbs are in the same form:

Painting with oils is easier than painting with watercolors.

As usual, you may encounter sentences with intervening, camouflaging clauses:

Painting with oils, which you might as well use if you want to paint at all, is easier than when you paint with watercolors.

Don't be thrown by a camouflaging clause. Change *when you paint* to *painting*, just as we did in the previous, incorrect sentence.

IDIOMS AND WORD CHOICE

You have a fairly good chance of seeing a few Writing section items that test proper use of vocabulary, or **usage**. For example, what's wrong with the following sentence?

The film had a powerful affect on me.

Affect is not the word you need; *effect* is correct. *Affect* as a noun means "emotion" or "mood"; *effect* as a noun means "an outcome or result." *Affect* as a verb means "to influence," whereas *effect* as a verb means "to cause to occur." A different example: *noisome* means "offensive smelling," not *noisy*.

There are many tricky pairs and triads in English. Whether you'll be faced with any particular one on the SAT is hard to predict. The best preparation is to sharpen your vocabulary. If you have some spare time, log on to **www.sparknotes.com/ultimatestyle** and check out our book *SparkNotes Ultimate Style* for a comprehensive list of commonly misused words.

Idioms are inherited quirks of language that we absorb without question but cause nonnative speakers endless trouble.

Here's an idiom we've all used:

It wasn't me.

Look at this grammatically. A pronoun that refers only to humans, *me*, is replacing a pronoun that refers only to inanimate objects, *it*.

Many idioms are meant to be taken figuratively. If you tell someone "I'm going to give you a piece of my mind," most likely you will walk away from the conversation with your brain intact. Idioms have no rhyme or reason to them: you simply have to know their meaning. Listing all possible idioms you might see on the SAT would take up the rest of this book and is a pretty low-yield investment strategy, since you won't see more than a couple of questions at most.

One particular type of idiom is more limited and more likely to be tested. The particular meaning of certain words requires the use of a particular preposition:

Incorrect: She prefers skiing over snowboarding.
Correct: She prefers skiing to snowboarding.

Incorrect: I don't have a favorable opinion toward Beethoven's music.
Correct: I don't have a favorable opinion of Beethoven's music.

Sometimes a word can be combined legitimately with more than one preposition, but the meaning will then shift. Knowing which preposition triggers which meaning is crucial to good usage:

My remark was <u>meant</u> **as** a joke.
You, my friend, are <u>meant</u> **for** greatness.

Meant as shows intent; *meant for* indicates a destination. A complete and relatively short list of such "prepositional idioms" can also be found in SparkNotes *Ultimate Style*.

Double Negatives

Finally, let's consider **double negatives**. When we want to negate something, we use *no* or *not*:

I allow **no** talking in my class.
I do**n't** allow any talking in my class.

For reasons of redundancy and idiomatic preference, we don't use *no* and *not* in the same sentences:

I do**n't** allow **no** talking in my class.

Words other than *no* and *not* can indicate negation. Here's a list of those words with their positive counterparts (which are not necessarily their **antonyms**). Don't use a negative word with *not* or *no*.

Negative Word	Positive Counterpart	Examples
never	ever	**Incorrect:** I don't never eat meat. **Correct:** I never eat meat. **Correct:** I don't ever eat meat.
none	any	**Incorrect:** I don't want none. **Correct:** I want none. **Correct:** I don't want any.
neither	either	**Incorrect:** I don't want neither of those two puppies. **Correct:** I want neither of those two puppies. **Correct:** I don't want either of those two puppies.
nor	or	**Incorrect:** I don't want the puppy nor the kitten. **Correct:** I want neither the puppy nor the kitten. **Correct:** I don't want the puppy or the kitten.
nothing	anything	**Incorrect:** I don't want nothing from you. **Correct:** I want nothing from you. **Correct:** I don't want anything from you.
no one	anyone	**Incorrect:** I can't help no one. **Correct:** I can help no one. **Correct:** I can't help anyone.
nobody	anybody	**Incorrect:** I don't know nobody here. **Correct:** I know nobody here. **Correct:** I don't know anybody here.

nowhere	anywhere	**Incorrect:** I can't go nowhere with this cast on my leg. **Correct:** I can go nowhere with this cast on my leg. **Correct:** I can't go anywhere with this cast on my leg.

Three other words are often involved in double negatives: *hardly*, *scarcely*, and *barely*.

> I can't hardly wait to get a new car. (Two negatives—*can't* and *hardly*)

Believe it or not, this is not grammatically incorrect, but it has fallen out of favor. The preferred versions are:

> I can hardly wait to get a new car. (One negative—*hardly*)
> I can't wait to get a new car. (One negative—*can't*)

ACTIVE VOICE AND PASSIVE VOICE

Voice is a feature of verbs that shows whether the subject of a sentence is doing the action or having the action done to it.

Passive: Parliament was not informed.
Active: The prime minister did not inform Parliament.

Note that the **passive voice** allows a writer or speaker to evade responsibility by hiding the identity of the person executing the action. "Gee, Parliament just wasn't informed. Isn't that unfortunate? What's next on the agenda?" The active version of the sentence names names and ascribes actions to a real, live person.

For that reason, the passive voice is most widely used in politics, the business world, or in any other activity involving a bureaucracy. Educators and stylists have been pushing for wider use of the active voice. The SAT reflects this trend. As you may have heard your English teacher say, *verb* your way through your writing. Use active, focused, forceful verbs, not the same weak passive verbs over and over again.

The **active voice** usually requires far fewer words than the passive voice to convey the same idea:

Passive : *The ball was thrown by the man to his son.* (10 words)
Active: *The man threw the ball to his son.* (8 words)

Passive: *The investigation of the war crimes alleged to have been committed by the occupying forces was carried out by an international agency.* (22 words)
Active: *An international agency led the investigation of the occupying forces' alleged war crimes.* (13 words)

Notice in both examples how we replaced a form of *to be* with a more active verb:

First example: *was* replaced by *threw*
Second example: *was* replaced by *led*

If you see a sentence that contains a form of *to be*, be on the lookout for an unnecessary passive construction.

Concision is the hallmark of good writing; the active voice is far leaner than the bloated passive voice. Paragraph Improvement sets often include passive constructions that need revision.

CLEAR AND CONCISE WRITING

Mastering the concepts already presented ensures that you will be able to recognize the great majority of the errors in Sentence Error ID, Sentence Improvement, and Paragraph Improvement items. However, Paragraph Improvement will also test your ability to recognize writing that is not as consistent, logical, or succinct as it could be. Primarily, you'll be directed to the connections between clauses, sentences, and paragraphs.

Let's demonstrate this higher-order level of error recognition and correction with a concrete example. Read the following poorly written paragraph. Keep in mind that this exercise is much harder than what the SAT Writing section actually tests.

Virgil's patron while he wrote the Aeneid *was Maecenas, a powerful minister and friend for Augustus, the all-powerful first emperor of Rome. The poet Virgil wrote beautiful, gorgeous Latin verse for all to see in the classic epic poem the* Aeneid *nineteen years before Christ was born. One of Maecenas's roles was to commission the production of works of art that would accrue glory to Augustus for purposes of justifying his new power. In the* Aeneid, *the fact that Virgil found in Homer's* Iliad *and* Odyssey *a foundation myth that connected Rome to Troy shows that the question as to whether Augustus based his political power on partly culturally recognizable myths is not wholly untrue. Connected the Julio-Claudian family into which Augustus had been adopted by Julius Caesar to Aeneas, son of the goddess Venus, who had escaped from burning Troy carrying his father on his back. Virgil follows Aeneas from Troy through his wanderings in the Mediterranean, to Carthage, and finally to Rome, where he founds a colony that eventually becomes Rome. While at Carthage, Aeneas falls in love with Queen Dido, but leaves her to found the people from which in spite of the fact of that love affair will spring the army that will raze Queen Dido's city to the ground some time later.*

This paragraph needs some serious work. We're going to fix it line by line.

(1) *Virgil's patron while he wrote the* Aeneid *was Maecenas, a powerful minister and friend for Augustus, the all-powerful first emperor of Rome.*

The above is not a lead sentence and starts the paragraph off in the middle—a typical Paragraph Improvement error.

Before finding a better home for this sentence, let's fix some redundancies. Note that *powerful* repeats. The adjective is applied to two different people, but we can do better. Also, if you're an emperor of Rome, aren't you already *all-powerful*? Finally, *a powerful minister and friend for Augustus* is awkward. Here's a fix:

During the *Aeneid*'s composition, Virgil's patron was Maecenas. As the trusted ally of Augustus, first emperor of Rome, Maecenas wielded great power on his friend's behalf.

(2) *The poet Virgil wrote beautiful, gorgeous Latin verse for all to see in the classic epic poem the* Aeneid *nineteen years before Christ was born.*

This is our topic sentence and should come first. For now, note again the redundancy of *beautiful, gorgeous*; of *poet, verse,* and *poem*; and of *nineteen years before Christ was born.* Also note the unnecessary phrase, *for all to see.* Here's a rewrite:

In 19 B.C., the Roman poet Virgil wrote some of the most beautiful Latin verse in his classic epic the *Aeneid*.

(3) *One of Maecenas's roles was to commission the production of works of art that would accrue glory to Augustus for purposes of justifying his new power.*

We can trim a lot of fat here. Don't ever allow any word to slack off. If a word isn't carrying its share of meaning, omit it. *Commission*, in this sense, means "order to be made," so *production* is redundant. *Works of art* can be cut down to simply *art*. The phrase *that would accrue glory to* might sound like highfalutin prose, but it's really just flab. And *for purposes of* should be avoided at all costs. Here's one possible rewrite:

One of Maecenas's roles was to commission art that would glorify Augustus's new regime.

(4) *In the* Aeneid, *the fact that Virgil found in Homer's* Iliad *and* Odyssey *a foundation myth that connected Rome to Troy shows that the question as to whether Augustus based his political power on partly culturally recognizable myths is not wholly untrue.*

First, phrases such as *the fact that* and *the question as to whether* should be avoided. Second, note the echo of *found* and *foundation*. Third, the adverb *partly* is misplaced. Fourth, *based on* is often used in a vague manner; surely there is another more forceful and specific verb we could use. Fifth, a culture cannot recognize a myth, so this too can be clarified. Sixth, this sentence implies, but doesn't make explicit, that Virgil's epic followed a propagandistic program that originated with Augustus but was executed by Maecenas. Finally, *not wholly untrue* introduces a logical problem that is best to cut. Note how *not wholly untrue* doesn't logically follow from *the question as to whether.* Can a question be found to be not wholly untrue? Avoid negative statements; they tend to be wordy and logically confusing. Here's one way to fix this sentence:

By appropriating material in Homer's *Iliad* and *Odyssey*, Maecenas's protégé constructed a foundation myth that traced Rome's origins to Troy. By aligning the emperor's new regime with a venerable and widely familiar myth, the *Aeneid* demonstrates one way in which Maecenas's commissions legitimized Augustus's power.

(5) *Connected the Julio-Claudian family into which Augustus had been adopted by Julius Caesar to Aeneas, son of the goddess Venus, who had escaped from burning Troy carrying his father on his back.*

This sentence, despite its length, is a fragment—there's no connection. Where's the subject? Furthermore, several potentially unfamiliar proper names are crammed into the sentence. Also, the tenses used are unnecessarily complex, which leads to chronological confusion. Examples of unnecessary information include Julius Caesar's adoption of Augustus and that *Aeneas escaped from burning Troy carrying his father on his back.* The technical name for Augustus's family (*Julio-Claudian*) is not critical either. Finally, this sentence fails to build upon the previous sentence in a crucial manner. It fails to present the genealogical connection between Augustus and Aeneas as a specific, legitimizing advantage of Virgil's more general genealogical connection between the people of Rome and Troy. Let's rewrite with these points in mind:

Moreover, Virgil specifically traced Augustus's lineage not only to the Trojan prince Aeneas but also to Aeneas's mother, the goddess Venus. Thus, Virgil granted Augustus kinship not only with a great sovereign of a venerable race but also with the gods themselves.

(6) *Virgil follows Aeneas from Troy through his wanderings in the Mediterranean, to Carthage, and finally to Rome, where he founds a colony that eventually becomes Rome.* (7) *While at Carthage, Aeneas falls in love with Queen Dido, but leaves her to found the people from which in spite of the fact of that love affair will spring the army that will raze Queen Dido's city to the ground sometime later.*

First, sentence 6 would be best used earlier in the paragraph, as it provides important information about the *Aeneid*'s plot that readers need in order to appreciate the main point of the paragraph: the epic's political value. However, it's not as concise as it could be. For example, *Rome* is mentioned twice. Also, Virgil doesn't *follow* Aeneas, his readers do. As the writer, Virgil is in control.

Virgil leads Aeneas from Troy across the Mediterranean to Carthage and finally to Italy, where he founds a colony that will eventually become Rome.

Second, given that the political value of the *Aeneid* is the paragraph's main point, we do not need to mention that Aeneas, progenitor of Rome, hooked up with Dido, ancestor of Carthage, an enemy Rome ultimately vanquished. The irony is not worth going off-topic for. Cut sentence 7 altogether, because it is riddled with redundancies (*the fact . . . that*; *raze . . . to the ground*), overly complex structure (*from which in spite of*), unclear chronology (*sometime later*), and vague identification of characters (we're not explicitly told that Dido was queen of *Carthage*).

Let's decide where to insert sentence 6 in the rewritten paragraph assembled below:

> In 19 B.C., the Roman poet Virgil wrote some of the most beautiful Latin verse in his classic epic the *Aeneid*. During the *Aeneid*'s composition, Virgil's patron was Maecenas. As the trusted ally of Augustus, first emperor of Rome, Maecenas wielded great power on his friend's behalf. One of Maecenas's roles was to commission art that would glorify Augustus's new regime. By appropriating material in Homer's *Iliad* and *Odyssey*, Maecenas's protégé constructed a foundation myth that traced Rome's origins to Troy. By aligning the emperor's new regime with a venerable and widely familiar myth, the *Aeneid* demonstrates one way in which Maecenas's commissions legitimized Augustus's power. Moreover, Virgil specifically traced Augustus's lineage not only to the Trojan prince Aeneas but also to Aeneas's mother, the goddess Venus. Thus, Virgil granted Augustus kinship not only with a great sovereign of a venerable race but also with the gods themselves.

With a few minor adjustments (highlighted below by plain text and ~~strikethroughs~~), the rewrite of sentence 6 would do nicely as the second sentence of this paragraph:

> In 19 B.C., the Roman poet Virgil wrote some of the most beautiful Latin verse in his classic epic the *Aeneid*. In that epic, a sequel to Homer's earlier *Iliad* and *Odyssey*, Virgil leads the Trojan prince Aeneas from ~~Troy~~ his besieged native city across the Mediterranean to Carthage and finally to Italy, where he founds a colony that will eventually become Rome. During the *Aeneid*'s composition, Virgil's patron was Maecenas. As the trusted ally of Augustus, first emperor of Rome, Maecenas wielded great power on his friend's behalf. One of Maecenas's roles was to commission art that would glorify Augustus's new regime. By appropriating material in Homer's *Iliad* and *Odyssey*,

Maecenas's protégé constructed a foundation myth that traced Rome's origins to Troy. By aligning the emperor's new regime with a venerable and widely familiar myth, the *Aeneid* demonstrates one way in which Maecenas's commissions legitimized Augustus's power. Moreover, Virgil specifically traced Augustus's lineage not only to ~~the Trojan prince~~ Aeneas but also to Aeneas's mother, the goddess Venus. Thus, Virgil granted Augustus kinship not only with a great sovereign of a venerable race but also with the gods themselves.

And the final, rewritten paragraph . . .

In 19 B.C., the Roman poet Virgil wrote some of the most beautiful Latin verse in his classic epic the *Aeneid*. In that epic, a sequel to Homer's earlier *Iliad* and *Odyssey*, Virgil leads the Trojan prince Aeneas from his besieged native city across the Mediterranean to Carthage and finally to Italy, where he founds a colony that will eventually become Rome. During the *Aeneid*'s composition, Virgil's patron was Maecenas. As the trusted ally of Augustus, first emperor of Rome, Maecenas wielded great power on his friend's behalf. One of Maecenas's roles was to commission art that would glorify Augustus's new regime. By appropriating material in Homer's *Iliad* and *Odyssey*, Maecenas's protégé constructed a foundation myth that traced Rome's origins to Troy. By aligning the emperor's new regime with a venerable and widely familiar myth, the *Aeneid* demonstrates one way in which Maecenas's commissions legitimized Augustus's power. Moreover, Virgil specifically traced Augustus's lineage not only to Aeneas but also to Aeneas's mother, the goddess Venus. Thus, Virgil granted Augustus kinship not only with a great sovereign of a venerable race but also with the gods themselves.

In an actual Paragraph Improvement set, as you will see, the task of revision is made considerably easier because the items are multiple choice. Rather than provide a revision, you'll only need to recognize both an error and its correction. Furthermore, when you write your essay, your main goal will be to *prevent* writing an essay as convoluted and error-ridden as the original version of the *Aeneid* essay.

It's time to learn the most efficient way to use your knowledge on testlike items and sets. We'll treat each of the item types separately. Let's begin with Sentence Error ID.

ESSENTIAL STRATEGIES

Now that you have the basics of language down, it's time to look at the item types on the new SAT.

TACKLING IDENTIFYING SENTENCE ERRORS

This item type only requires that you *recognize* a mistake—you don't have to fix it. Some items will be correct; most will have an error in one of their underlined sections. No item will have more than one error.

Here's the item you saw earlier:

1. <u>In Victorian</u> England, hunger and unemployment <u>was</u> so prevalent
       A   B

    that social revolution was a constant source of <u>anxiety for</u> members
                                                       C

    of the <u>upper class</u>. <u>No error</u>
           D   E

Note that, unlike most SAT items, which have both a stem and a set of answer choices, Sentence Error ID items embed their answer choices in their stems. There aren't many shortcuts you can use if you're stuck—in fact, there's only one: if you're sure that the sentence contains an error, but you can't isolate which underlined portion contains it, or you're running out of time, guess. You've already eliminated one answer choice— namely, **E**—so by guessing among the remaining four, you're ahead of the wrong-answer penalty.

That strategy aside, be sure to use the following step method *every* time you attempt a Sentence Error ID:

Step 1: Read the item carefully, noting the types of words or phrases that are underlined.

Step 2: **Ask yourself whether any underlined word or phrase, *in the context of the entire sentence*, is in error. Eliminate those that are correct.**

Step 3: **If you find no error, E is the correct answer.**

Perform step 3 only if you haven't identified an error in step 2.

Sentence Error ID in Slow Motion

In order to demonstrate exactly how this method works, let's attempt item 1 using our three-step method in slow motion.

Step 1: **Read the item carefully, noting the types of words or phrases that are underlined.**

1. <u>In Victorian</u> England, hunger and unemployment <u>was</u> so prevalent
       A   B

    that social revolution was a constant source of <u>anxiety for</u> members
                                                       C

    of the <u>upper class</u>. <u>No error</u>
           D   E

The essential concepts reviewed in the last section will give you an advantage. If you have some sense of what to look for, you can ignore the *noise* that the distractors represent and predict the kinds of errors you're likely to see. Likewise, if you note the kinds of words or phrases that are underlined, you will know what the SAT likes to test.

In this case, you have:

A	a prepositional phrase
B	a verb
C	another prepositional phrase
D	an adjectival phrase

Whether you identify these as formally as we did or simply think "*in*—that's a preposition; *was*—verb; *for*—another preposition; *upper*—adjective" does **not** matter. The key is not merely to identify but to *strategize* as follows:

Step 2: **Ask yourself whether any underlined word or phrase, *in the context of the entire sentence*, is in error. Eliminate those that are correct.**

The key here is that while an error will appear in an underlined portion of the sentence, in order to recognize the error, the function of that underlined portion must be considered as part of a whole. Do **not** judge the underlined portions in isolation from the sentence. We'll show you what we mean by this as we work through the answer choices below.

A   a prepositional phrase

You've learned that the SAT likes to test idioms. *In Victorian . . .* sounds wrong, but *In Victorian England . . .* sounds okay. Eliminate **A**. (Scratch a line through **A**'s part of the sentence, if you like.)

B   a verb

The SAT loves to test subject/verb agreement. Anytime you see a verb underlined, check out whether it agrees with the subject. What's the subject here? *Hunger and unemployment*? Bingo. A compound subject requires a plural verb. Choose **B**. Obviously, there's no need for step 3.

On the test, you'd just move on to the next item, but we'll review the other distractors to show you why they appeared.

C   another prepositional phrase

Again, think "idiom." *Anxiety for* sounds okay, especially when embedded in the phrase *a constant source of anxiety for*.

D   an adjectival phrase

There's no issue with comparatives versus superlatives here and no issue with adjective versus adverbs. We're familiar with *upper class*, so no problem.

Note how there was no way to judge if **B** (the verb, *was*) was right or wrong without determining its function within the sentence.

Guided Practice

Try this one on your own:

2.   Rita and Julie <u>are planning</u> to get <u>a doctorate</u> so that <u>they</u> can
                     A   B   C

become <u>professors</u>. <u>No error</u>
        D   E

Step 1: Read the item carefully, noting the types of words or phrases that are underlined.

Write down the type of word or phrase that is underlined in each of the spaces provided.

Choice	Type of Word or Phrase
A	
B	
C	
D	

Step 2: Ask yourself whether any underlined word or phrase, *in the context of the entire sentence*, is in error. Eliminate those that are correct.

Write whether you think there is an error and what type of error it is in each of the spaces provided.

Choice	Error?
A	
B	
C	
D	

Guided Practice Explanation

Step 1: Read the item carefully, noting the types of words or phrases that are underlined.

Choice		Type of Word or Phrase
A	*are planning*	plural verb
B	*a doctorate*	singular noun
C	*they*	plural pronoun
D	*professors*	plural noun

Step 2: Ask yourself whether any underlined word or phrase, *in the context of the entire sentence*, is in error. Eliminate those that are correct.

	Choice	Error?
A	*are planning*	This looks okay: a plural verb, *are planning*, that matches the compound subject, *Rita and Julie*.
B	*a doctorate*	This is singular but the subject is compound and therefore plural. Remember that nouns must match in number: *Rita and Julie* cannot earn **one** *doctorate*. **B** is correct.
C	*they*	Plural subject, plural pronoun. All is well here. Notice how the other underlined portions can focus your attention on the error.
D	*professors*	If *Rita and Julie* are becoming *professors*, why are they getting **one** *doctorate*?

Independent Practice

After you complete the following item, look on the following page for the explanation.

3. To <u>fundamentalist</u> movements around the globe, the nature of
        A

    modern societies <u>present</u> a <u>grave and permanent</u> threat to
            B   C

    traditional <u>ways of life</u>. <u>No error</u>
           D   E

Independent Practice Explanation

Step 1: Read the item carefully, noting the types of words or phrases that are underlined.

Choice	Type of Word or Phrase
A	adjective
B	plural verb
C	adjectival phrase
D	prepositional phrase

Step 2: Ask yourself whether any underlined word or phrase, *in the context of the entire sentence*, is in error. Eliminate those that are correct.

A seems fine—*fundamentalist movements* is unobjectionable. How about **B**? Note that *societies* is right next to *present*. This should immediately make you suspicious—remember "camouflaging clauses." The subject of this sentence is not *societies* but *the **nature** of modern societies*, which is singular and thus requires a singular verb. This is the error, so pick **B**. **C** is meant to distract the unsuspecting test-taker with what looks like a compound subject but is actually simply two adjectives. **D** is a familiar and correct prepositional idiom.

TACKLING IMPROVING SENTENCES

Unlike Sentence Error IDs, Sentence Improvements require not only that you recognize a mistake but also that you recognize how to fix it. Like Sentence Error IDs, some Sentence Improvements will have no error.

Here's the Sentence Improvement item you saw earlier:

1.   Eager to pass his final exams, <u>studying was the student's top priority</u>.

(A)   studying was the student's top priority.

(B)   the student made studying his top priority.

(C)   the top priority of the student was studying.

(D)   the student's top priority was studying.

(E)   studying was the top priority for the student.

Sentence Improvements look like the typical SAT item: the stem is followed by the answer choices. The correct answer will be the best choice from among the answer choices, "best" meaning the clearest and most precise statement available. The correct answer will *not* introduce a *new* error. This allows for a few backward strategies, which we'll soon present.

Use the following method *every* time you attempt a Sentence Improvement:

Step 1: Cover up the answer choices.

Step 2: Read the stem carefully and determine what type of word, phrase, or clause is underlined.

Step 3: Ask yourself whether the underlined portion, *in the context of the entire sentence*, is in error. If not, choose A.

Step 4: If there is an error, generate a potential fix *without* looking at the answer choices.

Step 5: Compare your fix to the answer choices and eliminate all those that do not match.

Step 6: Check your selection by plugging the answer choice's text into the original sentence.

Here are some important notes on each step of this method:

- **Step 1**: Remember that four of the answer choices are distractors. To undermine their effectiveness, ignore them until you have a good idea of what the fix should be. Get yourself a 3-by-5-inch index card to cover up the answer choices; using your hand is a bit cumbersome.
- **Step 2**: Again, the idea is **not** to waste time coming up with grammatical terminology but rather to use the names of the essential concepts you've mastered to help predict fixes.

- **Step 3**: Remember, context is critical. Every essential concept is important here: agreement, parallel structure, modification, and so on.
- **Step 4**: Having an idea of what the correct answer should be *before* looking at the answer choices undermines the distractors' effectiveness and saves you time.
- **Step 5**: Develop some flexibility when comparing your idea of the correct answer to the answer choices. Recall that some errors can be fixed in multiple ways, all of which are equally correct. Errors in parallelism are a good example of this phenomenon. *I like singing and to dance* can be corrected by writing *I like singing and dancing* or *I like to sing and to dance.*
- **Step 6**: Brisk movement through a section is important, but getting points is the goal. Balance speed with accuracy by taking a few seconds to test your potential selection by plugging it back into the stem.

Sentence Improvement in Slow Motion

Let's apply this method by attempting item 1 in slow motion, making all thought processes explicit.

Step 1: Cover up the answer choices.

We'll do this for you:

1. Eager to pass his final exams, <u>studying was the student's top priority</u>.

Step 2: Read the stem carefully and determine what type of word, phrase, or clause is underlined.

Studying was the student's top priority is a clause preceded by an introductory clause. Since the SAT just *loves* to test clause structure, you've isolated the likely category of error.

Step 3: Ask yourself whether the underlined portion, *in the context of the entire sentence*, is in error. If not, choose A.

Exactly who is *eager to pass his final exams, the student* or *studying*? We've got an error here! You can eliminate **A**.

Step 4: If there is an error, generate a potential fix *without* looking at the answer choices.

Put *the student* next to the introductory clause:

> Eager to pass his final exams, the student's top priority was studying.

Do not actually write down your potential fix, as doing so is almost certainly a waste of time. Scribble down the key point, if that helps. In this case: "the student's" might be all you'd need to jot down in the margin of your test book. Experience will dictate what works best for you in particular situations.

Step 5: Compare your fix to the answer choices and eliminate all those that do not match.

Now you can look at the answer choices:

(A)   studying was the student's top priority.
(B)   the student made studying his top priority.
(C)   the top priority of the student was studying.
(D)   the student's top priority was studying.
(E)   studying was the top priority for the student.

The answer is **D**. **B** looks okay, but it is less concise than **D**. Sometimes you'll predict the precise answer; other times you won't. For some errors, the fix is almost predetermined; for others, more than one potential fix will do. The more clauses in the item, the more likely it will be that more than one fix could apply.

Step 6: Check your selection by plugging the answer choice's text into the original sentence.

Always do this, even when certain of your answer. Gaining even one point on the SAT test will make this extra, split-second step worthwhile.

Sentence Improvement in Reverse: Backward Strategies

We'd like to point out a few important strategies that you can resort to when you're running out of time, or when you're just stumped:

Eliminated A? Guess Away! If you're sure something is wrong with the underlined portion of the sentence, but you're not quite sure of what it is, just guess! As with eliminating **E** in Sentence Error ID, eliminating **A** in

Sentence Improvement puts you ahead of the wrong-answer penalty.

Original Intent Remember that the correct answer cannot change the original meaning of the sentence. If you're stuck, eliminate any answer choices that change the original meaning in some way.

Read My Lips: No New Errors The correct answer *cannot* introduce a *new* error. If you don't know exactly what's wrong with a sentence, or cannot come up with a good prediction in a timely manner, eliminate any answer choices that contain a new error.

Groupthink A particularly useful strategy derives from how the SAT structures Sentence Improvement answer choices. Look at the following item again:

1. Eager to pass his final exams, <u>studying was the student's top priority</u>.

(A) **studying** was the student's top priority.
(B) **the student** made studying his top priority.
(C) **the top priority** of the student was studying.
(D) **the student's** top priority was studying.
(E) **studying** was the top priority for the student.

We've bolded the first word or two to highlight that Sentence Improvement answer choices tend to fall into discrete groups. It's unusual to see five totally different answer choices. **Grouping** makes the process of elimination all the more powerful because, if you can eliminate a group, you eliminate several answer choices in one fell swoop.

In this case, you have an introductory clause that may very well be a dangler: *Eager to pass his final exams*. Therefore your attention is already focused on what that clause should be modifying. You're choosing between:

A, E *studying*
B, D *the student*
C *the top priority*

If you notice this grouping feature of the answer choices, it can help you troubleshoot three different scenarios:

Scenario 1: Trouble with time

If you don't have the time to check all the possibilities, eliminate what you know to be wrong and guess from the remaining. For example, if you had decided that this sentence was in error, **A** would be automatically eliminated. Since **A** and **E** group, **E** is also eliminated. You've beaten the wrong-answer penalty, so guess away.

Scenario 2: Trouble identifying the error

If you're having trouble identifying the error in the stem (or whether there *is* an error in the stem), determining the answer-choice groupings can alert you to the potential error. In this case, the three groups of answer choices can help trigger your memory of the essential concept of dangling modifiers.

Scenario 3: Trouble predicting a fix

If you're having trouble predicting a fix, go to the answer choices and use grouping not only to trigger your memory of essential concepts but also to efficiently work backward, eliminating potential groups of answer choices in sequence.

The Ultimate Shortcut

A final, last-ditch strategy is simply to choose the *shortest* answer choice. This is often, but **not** always, the correct choice. Whether you deploy this strategy will be a matter of judgment while taking the test. The more you practice, the better your judgment will be.

We'll put these backward strategies in the context of handling Sentence Improvement sets and whole Writing sections later on in this book.

Let's do some practice.

Guided Practice

Try the following item on your own:

Step 1: Cover up the answer choices.

We'll do this for you:

2. <u>Tickets to see the veteran rock group's show were a hot commodity, this was the group's farewell tour.</u>

Step 2: Read the stem carefully and determine what type of word, phrase, or clause is underlined.

Write down the type of word, phrase, or clause.

Step 3: Ask yourself whether the underlined portion, *in the context of the entire sentence*, is in error. If not, choose A.

Write down whether you think there is an error and what type of error it is. In this case, the entire sentence is underlined. This occurs every so often on the test.

Step 4: If there is an error, generate a potential fix *without* looking at the answer choices.

Write down your potential fix.

Step 5: Compare your fix to the answer choices and eliminate all those that do not match.

Compare your potential fix to the answer choices provided below. Remember that you can use grouping and other backward strategies.

(A)   Tickets to see the veteran rock group's show were a hot commodity, this was the group's farewell tour.

(B)   Tickets to see the veteran rock group's show were a hot commodity this was the group's farewell tour.

(C)   Tickets to see the veteran rock group's show were a hot commodity. This was the group's farewell tour.

(D)   Tickets to see the veteran rock group's show were a hot commodity, this farewell tour was the group's last hurrah.

(E)   Tickets to see the veteran rock group's show were a hot commodity; this show was the last hurrah of the group's career.

Step 6: Check your selection by plugging the answer choice's text into the original sentence.

It's always worthwhile to do this.

Guided Practice Explanation

Step 1: Cover up the answer choices.

We did this for you.

Step 2: Read the stem carefully and determine what type of word, phrase, or clause is underlined.

For this item, you have two independent clauses (i.e., two clauses that could stand alone).

Step 3: Ask yourself whether the underlined portion, *in the context of the entire sentence*, is in error. If not, choose A.

At this point, warning indicators in your head should be flashing: "Clause structure! Clause structure!" while a calm, deep voice repeats: "Do not panic. Please proceed directly to the connection between the clauses."

Since it is not okay to join two independent clauses with a comma, there is an error here.

Step 4: If there is an error, generate a potential fix *without* looking at the answer choices.

Remember that if commas are pauses, and periods are full stops, then semicolons are somewhere closer to a period than a comma. Semicolons can connect independent clauses:

Tickets to see the veteran rock group's show were a hot commodity; this was the group's farewell tour.

Step 5: Compare your fix to the answer choices and eliminate all those that do not match.

Lift your 3-by-5-inch card to reveal:

(A)   Tickets to see the veteran rock group's show were a hot
        commodity, this was the group's farewell tour.
(B)   Tickets to see the veteran rock group's show were a hot
        commodity this was the group's farewell tour.
(C)   Tickets to see the veteran rock group's show were a hot
        commodity. This was the group's farewell tour.
(D)   Tickets to see the veteran rock group's show were a hot
        commodity, this farewell tour was the group's last hurrah.
(E)   Tickets to see the veteran rock group's show were a hot
        commodity; this show was the last hurrah of the group's career.

There are often many possible fixes. If your prediction isn't there, find an equivalent one in the choices.

In this case, **C** works just fine. Periods can also separate independent clauses.

Note, too, how the choices grouped:

A, D   Comma
B   No punctuation at all
C   Period
E   Semicolon

E is not incorrect but **C** is better. It is more succinct and active than **E**. Answer **E** uses correct punctuation, but it introduces the passive voice and unnecessary words (*the last hurrah*).

Given the many potential fixes and the various backward strategies that can be employed, you may find yourself alternating between the stem, your prediction, and the answer choices in the manner we just demonstrated. This is to be expected. As your proficiency with Sentence Improvements increases, you'll learn to alternate with increasing skill and speed.

Finally, take a moment to see the various ways in which you could have eliminated different groups of answer choices if you'd been stumped or pressed for time.

Step 6: Check your selection by plugging the answer choice's text into the
        original sentence.

Always do this, as it is worthwhile every time.

Independent Practice

After you complete the following item, look on the following page for the explanation.

2. For as long as she could remember, Brenda has loved <u>to paint, to knit, and, until her hearing loss made it impossible for her to do so,</u> listening to opera.

(A) to paint, to knit, and, until her hearing loss made it impossible for her to do so,

(B) painting, to knit, and, until her hearing loss made it impossible for her to do so,

(C) painting, knitting, and, until her hearing loss made it impossible for her to do so,

(D) to paint, to knit, and, until she lost her hearing,

(E) painting, knitting, and, until she lost her hearing,

Independent Practice Explanation

Step 1: Cover up the answer choices.

Always do this.

Step 2: Read the stem carefully and determine what type of word, phrase, or clause is underlined.

There is the beginning of a series here: *to paint, to knit, and* . . . There is also a subordinate clause, *until her hearing loss made it impossible for her to do so.*

Step 3: Ask yourself whether the underlined portion, *in the context of the entire sentence*, is in error. If not, choose A.

A series should trigger your memory of the essential concept of parallelism. Also, note the typical insertion of a camouflaging intervening clause. Don't let that fool you.

Step 4: If there is an error, generate a potential fix *without* looking at the answer choices.

Usually there would be two equivalent fixes for nonparallel series: all-infinitive or all-gerund. Note, however, that *listening to opera* is **not** underlined. That means it has to be taken as a given feature of any fixed sentence: it can't be changed, which rules out the all-infinitive option.

There is only one workable potential fix:

For as long as she could remember, Brenda has loved painting, knitting, and, until her hearing loss made it impossible for her to do so, listening to opera.

Step 5: Compare your fix to the answer choices and eliminate all those that do not match.

Here are those answer choices again:

(A)   to paint, to knit, and, until her hearing loss made it impossible for her to do so,

(B)   painting, to knit, and, until her hearing loss made it impossible for her to do so,

(C)   painting, knitting, and, until her hearing loss made it impossible for her to do so,

(D)   to paint, to knit, and, until she lost her hearing,

(E)   painting, knitting, and, until she lost her hearing,

C matches your prediction. But wait—note how the choices group:

A, D   *to paint . . .*
C, E   *painting, knitting . . .*
B   *painting, to knit . . .*

At this point, you already know that **A**, **B**, and **D** are out. But what about **E**? Don't be so married to your potential fix that you refrain from entertaining another answer choice that matches the key part of your potential fix.

  E, it turns out, is actually *better* than **C**. It's more concise, which counts for a lot on the SAT.

  Look again at step 2 in this explanation. We noted that there were actually *two* separate types of phrases in the underlined portion of the stem: the series and the subordinate clause. Also note how there is not one but *two* different ways to group the answer choices, each way tied to one of the two separate types of phrases in the underlined section:

First Grouping

A, D   *to paint . . .*
C, E   *painting, knitting . . .*
B   *painting, to knit . . .*

Second Grouping

A, B, C   *until her hearing loss made it impossible for her to do so,*
D, E   *until she lost her hearing,*

Compare the two groupings, and you will quickly whittle down to the best answer.

Again, we're purposely dragging out this explanation—in slow motion, so to speak—in order to make the thought processes totally clear. The more you practice, the faster you'll get.

Step 6: Check your selection by plugging the answer choice's text into the original sentence.

Will I always do this? Yes, you will. Is it always worthwhile to do so? Yes.

TACKLING IMPROVING PARAGRAPHS

Enough with the sentences, already! Let's sink our teeth into the paragraphs.

Unlike the sentence-level items, Paragraph Improvement items come in sets, which are best understood as minitests (or "testlets") within a larger test. All the items in the set are tethered to a poorly written passage. So before we do *anything* else, we need to address a long-standing debate in test preparation—over which much ink, if not actual blood, has been spilled—about how to handle passage sets. Here's the question that has unstaunched a thousand lips:

> *When confronted with passage sets, what should you do first:*
> *read the passage or go directly to the items?*

In the case of Paragraph Improvement sets, answering the items requires having first read the passage. (The exceptions are discussed later.) So, in most cases, use the following step method to handle Paragraph Improvement sets.

Step 1: Read the passage quickly to get the general idea. Circle or mentally note any errors you happen to see.

Step 2: Read *all* the item stems in the set.

Step 3: Decide which items are easiest and tackle those first. Leave the others for last.

Of course there is also an item-specific step method, which we will discuss later on.

Tackling the Passage in Slow Motion

Paragraph Improvement passages are poorly written by intent. As you saw in Essential Concepts, the passages are lacking, or "broken," in a limited number of ways. Most of the ways in which the passages are broken pertain to connections within, between, and among paragraphs—hence the name, "Paragraph Improvement."

In order to demonstrate the three-step set method, let's attempt the following set in slow motion.

Step 1: Read the passage quickly to get the general idea. Circle or mentally note any errors you happen to see.

For the purposes of this demonstration, we'll substitute **bolding** for circling.

> **(1) Japanese cuisine continues to grow in popularity in the United States. (2) Americans are already fond of Chinese food. (3) Now they are discovering that Japanese cuisine** takes a similar set of basic ingredients and transforms them into something quite special. **(4)** That Japanese food is generally low in fat and calories, and offers many options for vegetarians and vegans, adds to its popularity.
>
> **(5) Americans' enjoyment of Japanese cooking is still largely limited to an occasional night out at a Japanese restaurant. (6) Actually, Japanese cooking is surprisingly simple. (7)** Anyone with a standard set of cooking utensils and knowledge of basic cooking terms can easily follow the recipes in any Japanese cookbook.
>
> **(8)** Since Japanese restaurants tend to be fairly expensive, one would think that fans of the cuisine would be excited about the possibility of making it at home. **(9)** Unfortunately, many traditional Japanese recipes call for costly ingredients that often can only be found at Asian grocery stores. **(10)** As these ingredients become more widely available at lower prices, we are sure to see a proportional increase in the number of people cooking Japanese food at home.

The main gist of the passage is that while Japanese restaurants have become increasingly popular, home preparation of Japanese cuisine has not. The passage explains why this is the case, and why it may not be the case for much longer.

- **First bolding:** Sentence 1 is a nice opening sentence. However, as we read sentence 2 and then 3, things get a bit choppy. Since Paragraph Improvement primarily tests connections, you not only should be attuned to choppiness but also prepared to see at least one item that refers to this choppy bit of the passage.
- **Second bolding:** Something's missing here. *Actually* is the tip-off—a connecting word that compares sentence 6 to a phantom sentence. The paragraph jumped from Japanese restaurants to Japanese cooking, and it's stated that *Japanese cooking is surprisingly simple*—but in comparison to what? Much like Japanese food, this is fishy.

Step 2: Read *all* the item stems in the set.

As you'll soon see, pacing is crucial to success on timed standardized tests. If two people have identical content knowledge, identical familiarity with item types, and are armed with identical step methods and strategies, but only one of them knows how to pace herself, the one who understands pacing will get the higher score.

Paragraph Improvement sets are *testlets*, so treat them as you would any larger SAT section in which all items have equal value: do the easier ones first; leave the tougher ones for last.

Whereas some SAT item types are organized into sets based on a statistically determined order of difficulty (more on this later), Paragraph Improvement sets are not. Therefore, "easy" and "difficult" are entirely relative to you, the test-taker.

To choose the easy ones, you must read all the stems. Note that we said *stems*, not *items*—don't waste time reading all the answer choices; the stems will give you enough information.

Here are the stems:

1. In context, what is the best way to revise and combine sentences 2 and 3 (reproduced below)?

   Americans are already fond of Chinese food. Now they are discovering that Japanese cuisine takes a similar set of basic ingredients and transforms them into something quite special.

2. In context, what is the best word to add to the beginning of sentence 5?

3. What would be the best phrase to add to the end of sentence 5 to improve the transition to sentence 6?

4. What would be the best subject for a sentence inserted after sentence 7?

5. Which phrase best describes the purpose of the passage?

Step 3: Decide which items are easiest and tackle those first. Leave the others for last.

You don't have to spend time categorizing the exact order in which you'll tackle the items in the set. Doing it one-by-one is fine: Pick the easiest item, complete it, pick the next easiest item, complete it, and so on till you're done or time runs out. Keep in mind that it won't take you very long to read the stems. The time you'll save and points you'll gain tackling questions according to *your* order of difficulty will more than compensate for the minute or so you'll invest.

In order to give you an idea of the thought processes involved in this step, we'll categorize all five items at once in the following chart. Also, since this categorization is an individual one, these are merely one person's reasons. You don't need to agree with them—follow your own strengths and experiences. What we want you to absorb is the importance and efficiency of doing easy items first.

Order	Item	Reason
1st	5	Since I've read the passage for the main idea, and I think I got it, I might as well take care of this item first. I've already done all the work I need.
2nd	4	Again, I just read this passage. I don't think it will take much for me to insert a relevant idea in here.
3rd	2	This item turns on only one word. I'll bet I can determine quickly which one works best. A low investment for a point!
4th	1	I'll try this next because the two sentences are reproduced right there for me to use. I noticed the choppiness the first time through.
5th	3	This item will turn on a phrase. This may take more time; I'll leave it for last.

Remember that all the items are categorized at once for instructional purposes only. Decide one-by-one which item to tackle as you move through the set.

As noted, Paragraph Improvement sets have a variety of items—more, in fact, than are represented in this example. There isn't much point in dumping a list of subitem types on you, especially given that:

- You will become familiar with these items as you practice.
- All items can be tackled according to the step method that follows.
- There will be fewer Paragraph items than either Sentence Error IDs or Sentence Improvements, and all items are worth the same amount.

Tackling the Items in Slow Motion

Paragraph Improvement items will have the familiar stem-plus-answer-choice format. Many will look a lot like Sentence Improvement items. In fact, most of what we've said about Sentence Improvement items applies to their Paragraph Improvement cousins. One exception is that Paragraph Improvement items do not always repeat underlined portions as choice **A**. Paragraph Improvement answer choices also tend to group more loosely than their Sentence Improvement cousins, but they still group.

The items that don't resemble Sentence Improvements tend to ask about the main idea of the passage, or provide topics or sentences not in the original passage that might be included, and ask you whether or where you'd insert them.

Use the following method *every* time you attempt a Paragraph Improvement item:

Step 1: Cover up the answer choices.

Step 2: Read the stem carefully.

Step 3: If directed to the passage, go back and reread.

Step 4: Generate a potential fix or answer *without* looking at the answer choices.

Step 5: Compare your potential fix or answer to the answer choices and eliminate all that do not match.

Step 6: If applicable, check your selection by plugging the answer choice's text into the original sentence or the passage.

Since we're dealing primarily with the connections within, between, and among paragraphs—which are units of meaning far more complex than sentences—apply this method flexibly. Sometimes, for example, you'll need to read more than one sentence prior to and subsequent to the sentences referenced in the stem. But the basic idea remains the same: determine local context. You'll undermine your efforts by ignoring this method, but don't shackle yourself by being too literal about it.

Let's apply this method in slow motion to the items that follow. We'll adhere to the order of items determined above: **5**, **4**, **2**, **1**, and **3**. The first two are done for you. Then we'll help you with the next two. The last one is up to you.

(1) Japanese cuisine continues to grow in popularity in the United States. **(2)** Americans are already fond of Chinese food. **(3)** Now they are discovering that Japanese cuisine takes a similar set of basic ingredients and transforms them into something quite special. **(4)** That Japanese food is generally low in fat and calories, and offers many options for vegetarians and vegans, adds to its popularity.

(5) Americans' enjoyment of Japanese cooking is still largely limited to an occasional night out at a Japanese restaurant. **(6)** Actually, Japanese cooking is surprisingly simple. **(7)** Anyone with a standard set of cooking utensils and knowledge of basic cooking terms can easily follow the recipes in any Japanese cookbook.

(8) Since Japanese restaurants tend to be fairly expensive, one would think that fans of the cuisine would be excited about the possibility of making it at home. **(9)** Unfortunately, many traditional Japanese recipes call for costly ingredients that often can only be found at Asian grocery stores. **(10)** As these ingredients become more widely available at lower prices, we are sure to see a proportional increase in the number of people cooking Japanese food at home.

Step 1: Cover up the answer choices.

5.   Which phrase best describes the purpose of the passage?

Step 2: Read the stem carefully.

This is a "main idea" stem.

Step 3: If directed to the passage, go back and reread.

Step 3 is not applicable to this item.

Step 4: Generate a potential fix or answer *without* looking at the answer choices.

Determine the main idea of this passage: while Japanese restaurants have become increasingly popular, home preparation of Japanese cuisine has not, but this will soon change.

Step 5: Compare your potential fix or answer to the answer choices and eliminate all that do not match.

Here are the answer choices:

(A)   To encourage people to eat at Japanese restaurants more often.
(B)   To record America's increasing interest in ethnic food.
(C)   To predict a future increase in Japanese cooking in American homes.
(D)   To discourage people from eating unhealthy food.
(E)   To promote the purchase of expensive cooking equipment.

C matches our potential answer. Typical distractors (also found in Critical Reading passage sets) fall into a few categories:

A: Distortion. The passage encourages more home cooking.
B: Off-topic. Japanese cuisine is one type of ethnic food; Chinese is mentioned, but only in comparison to Japanese food's increasing popularity, which is catching up to Chinese food.
D: Distortion. Just because the passage mentions that Japanese cuisine's relative healthiness has added to its popularity doesn't mean that the passage's main idea is to discourage the eating of unhealthy food.
E: Double Distortion! Not only does the passage not promote this, but it also argues that even Japanese cuisine, which has pricey ingredients (at present), requires only the usual cooking utensils.

Since there is usually only one main idea item, don't worry too much about these distractor types.

Step 6: If applicable, check your selection by plugging the answer choice's text into the original sentence or the passage.

Step 6 is not applicable to this item.

Let's look at item 4.

Step 1: Cover up the answer choices.

4.   What would be the best subject for a sentence inserted after sentence 7?

Step 2: Read the stem carefully.

You are asked to provide a potential *topic* for a sentence, not the sentence itself.

Step 3: If directed to the passage, go back and reread.

To gain context, reread this portion and keep the main idea in mind:

> **(6)** Actually, Japanese cooking is surprisingly simple. **(7)** Anyone with a standard set of cooking utensils and knowledge of basic cooking terms can easily follow the recipes in any Japanese cookbook.
>
> **(8)** Since Japanese restaurants tend to be fairly expensive, one would think that fans of the cuisine would be excited about the possibility of making it at home.

Step 4: Generate a potential fix or answer *without* looking at the answer choices.

In the second paragraph the passage makes a claim that Japanese cooking is easier than most Americans think. Specifically, sentence 7 claims that *anyone* who can cook can *easily* follow the recipes in *any* Japanese cookbook. Well, that's a pretty strong claim to make without some proof. This would be the place to insert such proof. Since persuasive writing depends on clear assertions backed up by examples, don't be surprised to see similar items on the test.

If you find it hard to come up with a potential answer on the actual test, don't waste time! Go to the answer choices. However, the more often you do this, the more at the mercy of the distractors you'll be. When you practice, be strict about predicting an answer, as that is the only way you'll build up that much-needed skill.

Step 5: Compare your potential fix or answer to the answer choices and eliminate all that do not match.

Here are the answer choices:

(A)   The rising popularity of other ethnic cuisine
(B)   An example of a simple Japanese recipe
(C)   A summary of the points made so far
(D)   Data on the profitability of Japanese restaurants
(E)   Information on where to buy Japanese cooking utensils

B is what you need. Note how the distractors stem from a misapprehension of the main point of the passage or a distortion of specific points in the passage.

Why would the SAT include these distortions? Students are often so pressed for time that they will grab at any distractor that repeats information from the passage, like a drowning person grabs at a flotation device. This is exactly what you must avoid. The strategic point behind all this practice effort is: the more familiar you are with the content and structure of the SAT, and with the methods and strategies that "rationalize" the test and organize your approach, the less likely you are to panic and fall for the distractors.

Step 6: If applicable, check your selection by plugging the answer choice's text into the original sentence or the passage.

Step 6 is not applicable to this item.

Guided Practice

Now try the next two on your own.

Step 1: Cover up the answer choices.

We'll do this for you:

2.   In context, what is the best word to add to the beginning of sentence 5?

Step 2: Read the stem carefully.

Step 3: If directed to the passage, go back and reread.

Read what you think is necessary to generate a potential answer. We'll discuss our choice of what to read in the explanation.

(1) Japanese cuisine continues to grow in popularity in the United States. (2) Americans are already fond of Chinese food. (3) Now they are discovering that Japanese cuisine takes a similar set of basic ingredients and transforms them into something quite special. (4) That Japanese food is generally low in fat and calories, and offers many options for vegetarians and vegans, adds to its popularity.

(5) Americans' enjoyment of Japanese cooking is still largely limited to an occasional night out at a Japanese restaurant. (6) Actually, Japanese cooking is surprisingly simple. (7) Anyone with a standard set of cooking utensils and knowledge of basic cooking terms can easily follow the recipes in any Japanese cookbook.

(8) Since Japanese restaurants tend to be fairly expensive, one would think that fans of the cuisine would be excited about the possibility of making it at home. **(9)** Unfortunately, many traditional Japanese recipes call for costly ingredients that often can only be found at Asian grocery stores. **(10)** As these ingredients become more widely available at lower prices, we are sure to see a proportional increase in the number of people cooking Japanese food at home.

Step 4: Generate a potential fix or answer *without* looking at the answer choices.

Write down your potential answer.

Step 5: Compare your potential fix or answer to the answer choices and eliminate all that do not match.

Here are the answer choices:

(A)   Yet,
(B)   Moreover,
(C)   Predictably,
(D)   Fortunately,
(E)   Undoubtedly,

Step 6: If applicable, check your selection by plugging the answer choice's text into the original sentence or the passage.

Do this if you think it is applicable. We'll discuss our decision in the explanation.

Guided Practice Explanation

Step 1: Cover up the answer choices.

2.   In context, what is the best word to add to the beginning of sentence 5?

Step 2: Read the stem carefully.

You're adding a word to the beginning of a sentence—a connection word is required.

Step 3: If directed to the passage, go back and reread.

Notice how the phrase *in context* keeps coming up? That's why we suggest that you read "around" the sentence or sentences referenced in the stem. You will have already gathered the main idea from your initial reading. By reading around the referenced sentences, you'll zero in on the local context in question and be in a good position to suggest a potential fix or answer.

In this case, you're asked to link the first word in the first sentence of the second paragraph to the entire first paragraph. You should reread the first paragraph as well as this sentence.

(1) Japanese cuisine continues to grow in popularity in the United States. (2) Americans are already fond of Chinese food. (3) Now they are discovering that Japanese cuisine takes a similar set of basic ingredients and transforms them into something quite special. (4) That Japanese food is generally low in fat and calories, and offers many options for vegetarians and vegans, adds to its popularity.

(5) Americans' enjoyment of Japanese cooking is still largely limited to an occasional night out at a Japanese restaurant. (6) Actually, Japanese cooking is surprisingly simple. (7) Anyone with a standard set of cooking utensils and knowledge of basic cooking terms can easily follow the recipes in any Japanese cookbook.

Step 4: Generate a potential fix or answer *without* looking at the answer choices.

The first paragraph states that Japanese cuisine is becoming increasingly popular. Then sentence 5 shifts the argument. Despite what has just been stated, there is an important qualifier: it turns out that this popularity is limited to restaurants; Japanese home cooking isn't catching on in the same way. This is the local context.

Some connection words that show contrast and fit this sentence are *however*, *yet*, *nevertheless*, and *still*.

Step 5: Compare your potential fix or answer to the answer choices and eliminate all that do not match.

Here are the answer choices:

(A)   Yet,
(B)   Moreover,
(C)   Predictably,
(D)   Fortunately,
(E)   Undoubtedly,

A works. **B** shows continuation, not contrast. At this point in the passage, there's nothing predictable about Japanese home cooking's relative lack of popularity at all, so **C** is out. Nor is there anything fortunate about it, from the author's point of view—quite the contrary—so **D** is incorrect. For **E**, consider if such a claim can be made. The word doesn't fit. Often one answer choice is way out in left field. Eliminate the "left-field" choice and guess from among the remaining answer choices.

Step 6: If applicable, check your selection by plugging the answer choice's text into the original sentence or the passage.

It's applicable—do it!

More Guided Practice

Try the next one on your own.

Step 1: Cover up the answer choices.

We'll do this for you:

1.   In context, what is the best way to revise and combine sentences 2 and 3 (reproduced below)?

Americans are already fond of Chinese food. Now they are discovering that Japanese cuisine takes a similar set of basic ingredients and transforms them into something quite special.

Step 2: Read the stem carefully.

Pay particular attention to the excerpt from the passage.

Step 3: If directed to the passage, go back and reread.

Read what you think is necessary to generate a potential answer. We'll discuss our choice of what to read in the explanation.

> **(1)** Japanese cuisine continues to grow in popularity in the United States. **(2)** Americans are already fond of Chinese food. **(3)** Now they are discovering that Japanese cuisine takes a similar set of basic ingredients and transforms them into something quite special. **(4)** That Japanese food is generally low in fat and calories, and offers many options for vegetarians and vegans, adds to its popularity.
>
> **(5)** Americans' enjoyment of Japanese cooking is still largely limited to an occasional night out at a Japanese restaurant. **(6)** Actually, Japanese cooking is surprisingly simple. **(7)** Anyone with a standard set of cooking utensils and knowledge of basic cooking terms can easily follow the recipes in any Japanese cookbook.
>
> **(8)** Since Japanese restaurants tend to be fairly expensive, one would think that fans of the cuisine would be excited about the possibility of making it at home. **(9)** Unfortunately, many traditional Japanese recipes call for costly ingredients that often can only be found at Asian grocery stores. **(10)** As these ingredients become more widely available at lower prices, we are sure to see a proportional increase in the number of people cooking Japanese food at home.

Step 4: Generate a potential fix or answer *without* looking at the answer choices.

Write down your potential answer.

Step 5: Compare your potential fix or answer to the answer choices and eliminate all that do not match.

Here are the answer choices:

(A)   Americans are already fond of Chinese food, and have
       discovered that Japanese cuisine takes a similar set of basic
       ingredients and transforms them into something quite special.

(B)   Americans are already fond of Chinese food, and now discover
       that Japanese cuisine takes a similar set of basic ingredients
       and transforms them into something quite special.

(C)   Already fond of Chinese food, Americans are now discovering
       that Japanese cuisine takes a similar set of basic ingredients
       and transforms them into something quite special.

(D)   Already fond of Chinese food, having discovered that Japanese
       cuisine takes a similar set of basic ingredients and transforms
       them into something quite special, Americans like it.

(E)   Americans are already fond of Chinese food; however, they are
       discovering that Japanese cuisine takes a similar set of basic
       ingredients and transforms them into something quite special.

Step 6: If applicable, check your selection by plugging the answer
choice's text into the original sentence or the passage.

More Guided Practice Explanation

Step 1: Cover up the answer choices.

1.   In context, what is the best way to revise and combine sentences 2
      and 3 (reproduced below)?

      *Americans are already fond of Chinese food. Now they are
      discovering that Japanese cuisine takes a similar set of basic
      ingredients and transforms them into something quite special.*

Step 2: Read the stem carefully.

You're asked to revise *and* combine. Again, we're dealing with connections—this time within a paragraph (and between sentences). This will
be similar to Sentence Improvement.

Step 3: If directed to the passage, go back and reread.

If a stem contains an excerpt, the answer to the item is most likely contained in that excerpt. In this case, go with the excerpt, but check back
with the entire paragraph in step 6.

Step 4: Generate a potential fix or answer *without* looking at the answer choices.

> Americans are already fond of Chinese food. Now they are discovering that Japanese cuisine takes a similar set of basic ingredients and transforms them into something quite special.

You need a connection between these two sentences that links Americans' fondness for Chinese food to the burgeoning popularity of Japanese cuisine. The author is stating that what happened to Chinese food is now happening to Japanese food: Americans like Chinese food; they're liking Japanese food more and more.

Try the following connection:

> Already fond of Chinese food, Americans are discovering that Japanese cuisine takes a similar set of basic ingredients and transforms them into something quite special.

We swapped *Americans are* with *already fond of Chinese food* in the first sentence and connected it with the second sentence by substituting *Americans* for *they* in the second sentence. In the original, *they* refers to *Americans*, so we fused the sentences by substituting the pronoun's antecedent for the pronoun itself. Once those two changes are made, the rest of the sentence—*discovering that Japanese cuisine takes a similar set of basic ingredients and transforms them into something quite special*—follows unchanged.

It's okay if you didn't come up with this potential fix, but pay attention to *how* we came up with this fix. The essential concepts will lead you to potential fixes; practice will make generating fixes second nature.

Step 5: Compare your potential fix or answer to the answer choices and eliminate all that do not match.

Here are the answer choices:

(A)   Americans are already fond of Chinese food, and have
        discovered that Japanese cuisine takes a similar set of basic
        ingredients and transforms them into something quite special.

(B)   Americans are already fond of Chinese food, and now discover
        that Japanese cuisine takes a similar set of basic ingredients
        and transforms them into something quite special.

(C)   Already fond of Chinese food, Americans are now discovering
        that Japanese cuisine takes a similar set of basic ingredients
        and transforms them into something quite special.

(D)   Already fond of Chinese food, having discovered that Japanese
        cuisine takes a similar set of basic ingredients and transforms
        them into something quite special, Americans like it.

(E)   Americans are already fond of Chinese food; however, they are
        discovering that Japanese cuisine takes a similar set of basic
        ingredients and transforms them into something quite special.

Our choice is **C**, and note that these answer choices group, just as Sentence Improvement choices do.

A, B, E   *Americans are . . .*
C, D   *Already fond of . . .*

If you had trouble coming up with a potential fix, or if you were pressed for time, let these groups guide you. At worst, you could eliminate some answer choices, guess, and move on.

Step 6: If applicable, check your selection by plugging the answer
        choice's text into the original sentence or the passage.

As a check, plug this new sentence into the original paragraph to make sure *context* isn't harmed in any way.

Sometimes, but not often, the most efficient and succinct solution *will not* work when substituted back into the larger structure of the paragraph or passage. So it's always worth a quick check.

Independent Practice

After you complete the following item, look at the following page for an explanation.

3. What would be the best phrase to add to the end of sentence 5 to improve the transition to sentence 6?

(A) , because people do not like to eat ethnic food on a regular basis.

(B) , and this has led to many restaurant closings.

(C) , because Americans have long assumed that Japanese cooking is too difficult for them.

(D) , because the recent economic recession has forced people to reduce their spending.

(E) , and this means that Japanese cuisine may disappear from America entirely.

Independent Practice Explanation

Something crucial is missing here, as we noted when we first read the passage together. We need a reason for why Americans' appreciation of Japanese food is confined to restaurants. The next sentence contains a clue: *Actually . . . surprisingly simple* needs to be contrasted with "something hard about Japanese cooking." That's your quick-and-dirty-but-good-enough potential fix: "something hard about Japanese cooking." No need to get any fancier than what works.

Compare your potential answer to the choices. **C** jumps right out as the correct answer. Check it by plugging it back into the sentence and passage.

The other answers either contradict the main idea of the passage (**B**, **E**) or have no basis in the passage (**D**, **A**).

BOMBING RUNS

Here's the order in which you should tackle the Writing section:

1. Do all Sentence Error IDs.
2. Do all Sentence Improvements.
3. If you have time, do all Paragraph Improvements.

This way, you'll start with the lowest-investment items and end (if time permits) with the highest-investment items. Since all items are worth one point, it's a good investment strategy.

Some item sets, such as Sentence Completions, are organized by order of difficulty from easiest to hardest. An item's "difficulty" is a statistical quality based on the test-takers who encountered that item in an experimental section. Writing section item sets are *not* organized by order of difficulty.

However, you should not attempt each item as presented, starting with the first and ending with the last. Within the three item-type sets, you should skip around. The key is to distribute your knowledge and skills as efficiently as possible to get the most points in the least amount of time. In order to maximize your points on the multiple-choice portion of the Writing section, follow what we call "Bombing Runs."

To illustrate this method, assume your set has ten items. Begin by reading the first stem. If it seems easy, complete the item and move on to the next stem. If you encounter a challenging stem, skip that item. (Make sure to circle the entire item in your test booklet if you skip it. Also, enter answers in five-item blocks, omitting whichever you've skipped. You don't want to misgrid your answers.) After completing all the items that are easy for you, return to those items that you could probably figure out, given a little more time. Make another Bombing Run, skipping all of the really tough ones. Repeat your Bombing Runs until time expires.

(For those who read the Paragraph Improvement sections, you've already seen bombing runs in action within those "testlets." Apply the same idea to each item set.)

If you approach Writing sets this way, you won't waste several minutes worrying over any particular item when you could be using that time to answer four other items. That's the principal error in standardized test-taking: wasting time on items you have little chance of getting right. You need to develop a fine-tuned sense of when to pass on any given item. In order to develop this sense, you need to practice. Through practice, you'll not only learn more about the test and become an expert at applying the methods you've learned, but you'll also learn more about your own strengths and weaknesses. Whether it is the items testing clause structure that are toughest for you or dangling modifiers, the more you practice, the more you'll learn and the more confident you'll be about the test and yourself.

THE 14 MOST COMMON MISTAKES

As you prepare, keep the following common mistakes in mind. Some apply to all three item types; others are more specific.

ALL THREE ITEM TYPES

1. Looking at the answer choices without having some idea of what the correct answer should be.
2. Spending more than a minute or so on any one item in a set.
3. Failing to practice sufficiently—*reading* this book is not enough!
4. Failing to master the Essential Concepts.
5. Failing to master the Essential Strategies.
6. Failing to practice the step methods on every practice test item—you'll need these methods when the answer *isn't* obvious to you.
7. Refusing to guess when you've eliminated one answer choice.
8. Refusing to fly Bombing Runs—that is, not doing items out of order based on your assessment of which will be easiest.
9. Having unrealistic expectations about your score goal. (Unless you're either already scoring fairly high on the Writing section or you have a lot of time before your test, spending time preparing for Paragraph Improvement will dilute your potential score payoff.)
10. If you've prepared for Paragraph Improvement, not doing all sentence-level items *before* attempting Paragraph Improvement.

SENTENCE ERROR IDS

11. Wasting time second-guessing yourself about whether an item contains an error. (If you don't see an error, choose **E** and move on.)

SENTENCE IMPROVEMENT

12. Not taking advantage of backward strategies, especially grouping.

PARAGRAPH IMPROVEMENT

13. Attempting any of these items *before* you've completed *all* the Sentence Error IDs and Sentence Improvements you can. (Since Paragraph Improvement sets contain a passage, this item type is a high investment for the same yield. All Writing section items are worth one point.)
14. Not treating Paragraph Improvement sets as a testlet (i.e., not flying bombing runs).

CONCLUSION

Without practice, you won't master the Multiple-Choice Writing section. You've learned quite a bit since you picked up this little book, but now comes the hard part—you have to apply it to testlike items. You'll find several practice sets at the end of this book. Here are some tips for getting the most out of these items:

- **Do not time yourself on the first Sentence Error ID, Sentence Improvement, or Paragraph Improvement set.** When you begin, don't worry about time at all. Take as long as you need to work through each set.
- **Read the explanations for all items, regardless of whether you got them right or wrong.** This last part is critical—always read *all* the explanations for each set's items. The idea is to develop skills that help you score points as quickly as possible. Most important, scoring a point doesn't mean you got it in the most efficient manner. The overarching goal is to apply the methods you've learned. Whether you get all, some, or none of the practice items right doesn't matter.

After the first set, start paying attention to time. Certainly by the actual test, give yourself only a minute or so per item.

ADDITIONAL ONLINE PRACTICE

Once you're done working through the items and explanations in this book, you can practice further by going online to **testprep.sparknotes.com** and taking full-length SAT tests. These practice tests provide you with instant feedback, delineating all your strengths and weaknesses.

Also, be sure to take the free multiple-choice writing posttest to see how well you've absorbed the content of this book. For this posttest, go to **testprep.sparknotes.com/powertactics**.

OTHER WAYS TO PREPARE

If you are not a reader, become one. Reading top-notch prose and learning by example is one of the most important (and pleasant) ways to become a good writer. Read literary fiction and magazines or newspapers with high-quality writing, such as the *New York Times*, the *Wall Street Journal*, *Scientific American*, *Harper's*, the *Atlantic Monthly*, the *Nation*, and the *Economist*. Many of these publications are available for free on the Internet.

Avoid reading "markety" language, which is often incorrect. Also, nothing beats learning by doing. In your day-to-day writing, whether in assignments for school or emails to friends, strive to be exact and correct in your grammar, logic, and choice of words. Correct does not mean stilted and boring.

Plan out a schedule of study not only for multiple-choice writing but also for all aspects of your SAT preparation. Having a plan and working day by day is the best antidote for anxiety. Preparing for the SAT does not have to be a nightmare. In fact, a positive attitude about the test will help focus your attention on maximizing your potential.

AND FINALLY . . .

In preparing for multiple-choice writing, you're also laying the groundwork for success on the essay. Sentence-level items test sentence-level writing skills *passively*. Paragraph Improvement sets build on these skills, *passively* testing the arrangement of sentences within paragraphs and the arrangement of paragraphs within passages. The essay will provide you with an opportunity to *actively* apply your language skills.

Much like musical proficiency, writing proficiency depends on having good role models (listen to the greats; read only the best writing), cultivating top-notch skills, and practice, practice, practice.

On to the practice items!

THE PRACTICE
SETS

SET 1: SENTENCE ERROR ID

1. If one <u>intends</u> to <u>excel in</u> a particular profession, <u>you</u> may <u>have to</u>
    A   B   C   D
    invest many years in specialized education. <u>No error</u>
    E

2. The cat is becoming <u>so popular</u> in <u>American homes</u> that <u>they</u> will
    A   B   C
    <u>soon</u> overtake the dog as America's favorite pet. <u>No error</u>
    D   E

3. No matter how <u>conscientious</u> you brush your teeth, <u>you</u> should
    A   B
    still <u>go</u> to a dentist for regular <u>cleanings</u>. <u>No error</u>
    C   D   E

4. The lightning bolt is such a <u>dramatic</u> symbol of power that <u>they</u>
    A   B
    are often found <u>in</u> mythology in connection <u>with</u> ruling deities.
    C   D
    <u>No error</u>
    E

5. <u>All</u> universities impose penalties <u>on</u> students who do not cite
    A   B
    sources <u>when</u> <u>he or she uses</u> other people's ideas. <u>No error</u>
    C   D   E

6. <u>The</u> social sciences are fast <u>becoming</u> the most popular <u>majors</u>
    A   B   C
    for undergraduate students <u>at</u> top universities in Europe.
    D
    <u>No error</u>
    E

7. The <u>effects of</u> global warming <u>have been studied</u> for years, but it
    A   B
    is only <u>recently</u> that <u>it has</u> begun to impact human lives.
    C   D
    <u>No error</u>
    E

8. The <u>appeal of</u> holiday cruises <u>depend</u> upon the quality of the
          A   B

    staff, <u>who serve</u>, entertain, and accommodate <u>the passengers</u>.
            C   D

    <u>No error</u>
      E

9. Most of the fans only <u>show up</u> to the baseball games <u>when</u> there
                            A   B

    are <u>hardly no</u> other events to attend <u>in the town</u>. <u>No error</u>
        C   D   E

ANSWERS & EXPLANATIONS

1. C

The sentence opens with the word *one* as the subject. Remember that it is acceptable to use either *one* or *you* as a subject, but it is incorrect to use both words in the same sentence. The second half of the sentence violates this rule by switching from *one* to *you* in choice **C**; this is the error you are looking for and the answer to the question. The verb *intends* in choice **A** correctly agrees with its subject; *one* is third person singular, and *intends* is the third-person singular conjugation of the verb *to intend*. The idiomatic phrase, *excel in*, choice **B**, is also without error. To *excel in* something means to be particularly good at something; the sentence makes the point that being particularly good at something requires many years of focused study. The idiom *have to* in choice **D** is also without error; the sentence demonstrates the necessity of studying for *many years* to become very good at *a particular profession*.

2. C

The sentence is trying to show just how popular *the cat is becoming*; the cat is *so popular*, choice **A**, that it will soon be more popular than the dog. The use of the phrase *so popular* is without error and sets up the rest of the sentence, where it will show to what degree cats have become popular. Where is the cat becoming so popular? In *American homes*, choice **B**. The word *American* is correctly put in is adjectival form to modify the noun *homes*. The pronoun *they*, choice **C**, refers back to the original subject of the sentence, which is *the cat*. Notice that while the word *cat* is singular, *they* is plural. Remember that a pronoun must agree in number with the noun it refers to. Choice **C** contains a grammatical error and therefore is the answer you are looking for. Choice **D**, *soon*, tells us when the sentence expects the cat to overtake the dog in popularity; there is no error here.

3. **A**

The word *conscientious*, choice **A**, modifies *brush*, which is a verb. Remember, a verb must be modified by an adverb; however, the word *conscientious* is an adjective. Choice **A** is not grammatically correct and therefore is the answer to this question. The pronoun *you*, choice **B**, is used consistently as the subject throughout both halves of the sentence. The verb *go*, choice **C**, agrees with its subject, *you*, choice **B**. Finally, *cleanings*, choice **D**, is the noun form of the verb *to clean* and functions correctly as the object of the preposition *for*.

4. **B**

The adjective *dramatic*, choice **A**, correctly modifies *symbol*, which is a noun; all nouns must be modified by adjectives. The pronoun *they*, choice **B**, refers back to the original subject of the sentence, *bolt*. Note that *bolt* is singular; the pronoun *they* is plural. The subject of the sentence and the referring pronoun do not agree with each other in number. Choice **B** contains an error and is the answer to this question. The preposition *in*, choice **C**, is utilized correctly; it lets you know that the author is making his or her point according to the world of *mythology*. The preposition *with*, choice **D**, is an idiom used in conjunction with the word *connection* and is intended to clearly point out that *lightning bolts* are often associated with *ruling deities* in the world of *mythology*.

5. **D**

The sentence opens with the adjective *all* correctly modifying the noun *universities*. The idiomatic preposition *on* in choice **B** is also used correctly; an institution or an authority figure *imposes* a penalty *on* someone else. The word *when*, choice **C**, is also without error; it tells us under what conditions *all universities* place *penalties on* students. However, the phrase *he or she uses*, choice **D**, is problematic; it is supposed to refer back to the word *students*. Note that while the word *students* is plural, *he or she* are both singular pronouns; a pronoun must always agree in number with its subject. To be correct, *he or she uses* needs to be replaced by *they use*. Choice **D** therefore contains the error in this sentence.

6. **E**

The article *the* correctly modifies the phrase *social sciences* in choice **A**; the sentence discusses a particular subject, *social sciences*. The main verb in the sentence, *are*, is modified by the present participle *becoming*, choice **B**. The sentence makes the point that *the social sciences are becoming*—in other words, are in the process of becoming—*the most popular majors*. The noun *majors*, choice **C**, refers back to *the social sciences*; the sentence tells us exactly what the *social sciences* are in the process of *becoming*. Both *social sciences* and *majors* are plural; they agree with each other in number. This means that choice **C** has no error. The preposition *at*, choice **D**, is also correct; its function in the sentence is to provide us with a context where *social sciences* are becoming most *popular*. There are no grammatical errors in this sentence, which makes choice **E** the correct answer.

7. **D**

The phrase *effects of*, choice **A**, is used without error; the sentence is going to tell us more about the results of global warming. The verb in the phrase *have been studied*, choice **B**, is intended to agree with the subject of the sentence, *effects*. Since *effects* is plural, and *have been* is also plural, the subject and verb agree with each other, and choice **B** contains no error. Choice **B** may have tempted you, however, if you thought that the subject of the sentence was *global warming*. Note, however, that *global warming* is located in a prepositional phrase, starting with the word *of*. This prepositional phrase simply modifies the true subject of the sentence, *effects*. In other words, the phrase *of global warming* tells us the kind of *effects* the author is going to discuss in the sentence; *global warming* alone is not the actual subject. The adverb *recently*, choice **C**, is grammatically correct, specifically pointing out at what point the *effects of global warming* have started to impact *human lives*. The pronoun *it* in choice **D** refers back to the subject of the sentence, which, remember, is the word *effects*. Notice that while the subject, *effects*, is plural, the pronoun, *it*, is singular. Recall that a pronoun must always agree in number with the noun it is referring to. To be correct, the word *it* in choice **D** would need to be replaced by the pronoun *they*. As a result, choice **D** contains a grammatical error and is the correct answer to this question.

8. **B**

Choice **A** contains the subject of the sentence: *appeal*. It is followed by the preposition *of*, signaling that the sentence is about to modify the subject and tell us specifically what kind of *appeal* we will learn more about in the course of the sentence. There is no error here. However, the verb *depend* in choice **B** is the main verb of the sentence and is supposed to agree with the subject; it does not. To be correct, the word *depend* would need to be changed to *depends*. Choice **B** therefore contains the error in the sentence and is the correct answer to the question. The phrase *who serve*, choice **C**, correctly modifies exactly what the *staff* do during *holiday cruises*. *The passengers*, choice **D**, are the object of the serving, entertaining and accommodating.

9. **C**

The subject of this sentence is the word *most*, which requires a third person plural verb. Choice **A**, *show up*, contains the verb of the sentence, which agrees with the subject. There is no error here. The adverb *when* in choice **B** tells us under which conditions *most fans* show up to *baseball games*; this is also without error. The word *hardly*, choice **C**, is a negative word. Using the word *hardly* along with another negative word, *no*, creates a double negative. The sentence is trying to say that *most fans show up* to *baseball games* when there are almost no other *events to attend*. The double negative used here negates the intention of the sentence. This makes choice **C** grammatically incorrect and the correct answer to the question. To be grammatically correct, tthe word *no* in choice **C** would need to be replaced with the word *any*. The prepositional phrase *in the town* in choice **D** tells us where the *fans* and the *baseball games* are located and is used without error.

SET 2: SENTENCE IMPROVEMENT

1. Because he was late to the <u>party was the reason the guest felt awkward when he was introduced to the host.</u>

    (A) party was the reason the guest felt awkward when he was
        introduced to the host.
    (B) party; the guest felt awkward being introduced to the host.
    (C) party, the guest felt awkward when he was introduced to the
        host.
    (D) party, the guest was feeling awkward when to the host he
        was introduced.
    (E) party; and the guest was feeling awkward when he was
        introduced to the host.

2. Having been an avid fan of music for most of her <u>life, the elderly woman found learning to play the piano very easy.</u>

    (A) life, the elderly woman found learning to play the piano very
        easy.
    (B) life, learning to play the piano came very easily to the
        elderly woman.
    (C) life; the elderly woman was able to learn to play the piano
        very easily.
    (D) life, it was very easy for the elderly woman to learn to play
        the piano.
    (E) life, and the elderly women found learning to play the piano
        very easy.

3. Jane Austen's novels are widely <u>read and they are studied every year</u> in universities throughout the world.

    (A) read and they are studied every year
    (B) read; they are studied every year
    (C) read, every year they are studied
    (D) read; and every year they are studied
    (E) read and studied, every year

4. In addition to being highly regarded as a bandleader, <u>Duke Ellington is also admired as one of the world's finest jazz pianists.</u>

    (A) Duke Ellington is also admired as one of the world's finest jazz pianists.
    (B) people also admire Duke Ellington as one of the world's finest jazz pianists.
    (C) Duke Ellington was also one of the world's finest jazz pianists, and as such is admired.
    (D) the world's finest jazz pianist; Duke Ellington, also is admired.
    (E) Duke Ellington, also is admired as one of the world's finest pianists.

5. The traveling circus made stops at small towns <u>that were all over the country during the last two years.</u>

    (A) that were all over the country during the last two years.
    (B) throughout the country during the last two years.
    (C) over the last two years that were all over the country.
    (D) all over the country that were during the last two years.
    (E) that were during the last two years all over the country.

6. The boxing champion is <u>almost as skillful leading with his left hand as he is leading with his right.</u>

    (A) almost as skillful leading with his left hand as he is leading with his right.
    (B) as skillful leading with his left hand, almost as he is with his right.
    (C) as skillful leading with his left hand as he is with his right almost.
    (D) with his left hand almost as skillful as he is leading with his right.
    (E) is leading almost as skillfully with his left as his is leading with his right.

7. <u>The weather, which was cold, made boating on the river</u> an unappealing activity that morning.

    (A) The weather, which was cold, made boating on the river
    (B) The weather, which being cold, was making boating on the river
    (C) Being cold, the weather on the river made boating
    (D) Boating was, being that the weather was cold,
    (E) The cold weather made boating on the river

8. An education is a difficult thing to <u>buy; only through hard work can one really learn.</u>

    (A) buy; only through hard work can one really learn.
    (B) buy, but one can only learn through hard work, really.
    (C) buy; but, through hard work, one can really only learn.
    (D) buy, only hard work lets one learn.
    (E) buy, through only hard work can one really learn.

9. It is difficult to tell if the employees were promoted because someone appreciated their intelligence or <u>because they liked the way they worked hard.</u>

    (A) because they liked the way they worked hard.
    (B) the reason being that they worked hard.
    (C) because someone liked the way they worked hard.
    (D) because the way the employees worked hard was appreciated.
    (E) that the reason was they liked their hard work.

ANSWERS & EXPLANATIONS

1. **C**

This sentence begins with the clause *because he was late to the party.* This is a dependent clause, and needs to be followed by a complete sentence. However, the second half of the sentence reads *was the reason the guest felt awkward when he was introduced to the host.* This is not a complete sentence; you need to find some way to make the second half of the sentence complete. Choice **A** will merely restate the original sentence and therefore cannot be correct. Choices **B** and **E** attempt to fix the problem by merging both halves of the sentence together with a semicolon. Recall that you can use a semicolon only if the two sentences on either side are complete. But you already know that the first half of the sentence is incomplete. Choice **D** has a host of problems. The phrase *when to the host he was introduced* is awkward and wordy. A much better solution is choice **C**, which makes clear that *the guest* was *late to the party* and *felt awkward when he was introduced to the host.*

2. **A**

The phrase *having been an avid fan of music for most of her life* modifies the subject, *the elderly woman.* There are no problems here. In the second half of the sentence, you learn that the same elderly woman found *learning to play the piano very easy*. The subject and verb agree with each other, and the sentence as a whole conveys a complete thought. There are no errors and the correct answer is choice **A**. Choice **B** changes the subject of the sentence from *the elderly lady* to *learning*, which makes it sound as though *learning* was an *avid fan of music for most of her life*, which is not very logical. Similarly, choice **D** changes the subject of the sentence from *the elderly woman* to *it*, which also obscures who or what was an *avid fan of music*. Choice **C** replaces the comma separating the two halves of the sentence with a semicolon. However, a semicolon should only be used to combine two complete sentences; the first half of the sentence is a clause and cannot stand alone. Choice **E** unnecessarily complicates and rearranges words.

3.   B

This sentence is made up of two independent clauses. On the one hand, you know that *Jane Austen's novels are widely read*. You are also told that *they are studied every year in universities throughout the world*. To combine these two independent clauses, you need to make one of the clauses dependent, using a conjunction like *and* or *but* and insert a comma, or use a semicolon. In this case, the two clauses are separated by the word *and*, but without a comma. Choice **A** is therefore incorrect. Scanning the answer choices, you should see right away that choices **B** and **D** use semicolons. However, choice **D** uses a semicolon and retains the conjunction *and*. Remember, you can only use a semicolon to separate two complete sentences; choice **D** cannot be the correct answer. Choice **B**, however, removes the conjunction *and*. Both halves of the sentence are complete; this is the correct answer. Choice **C** removes *and* and puts in a comma; this creates a run-on sentence. Choice **E** puts the comma in *after studied*, but this merely makes the second half of the sentence, *every year in universities throughout the world*, incomplete and therefore incorrect.

4.   A

Duke Ellington is the main subject of the sentence. The modifying phrase *in addition to being highly regarded as a bandleader* is immediately followed by the subject, Duke Ellington. This is the correct placement of both the modifier and the subject, leaving no confusion. A comma also correctly sets off the modifying phrase. The opening phrase *in addition to* signals that you are going to learn something else about Duke Ellington; in fact, he is *one of the world's finest jazz pianists*. There are no errors here, so choice **A** is the correct answer to the question. Choice **C** creates unnecessary wordiness by inserting the clumsy phrase *and as such is admired* at the end of the sentence. Choice **D** also complicates things by changing the subject of the sentence from *Duke Ellington*, to *the world's finest jazz pianist*. Choice **B** really creates confusion; *people* becomes the subject. This is problematic because the sentence reads as though *people* are *highly regarded as a bandleader*. Choice **E** garbles the words so badly, the entire sentence ceases to be complete and is instead a fragment.

5. **B**

The modifying clause *that were all over the country during the last two years* is intended to modify *small towns*. The wording is awkward and makes it sound as though small towns *were all over the country*—as though the small towns were moving around, which makes little logical sense. You know what the author is trying to say—but there must be a clearer way to demonstrate the placement of the small towns. Choice **C** makes things worse by separating the modifying clause *that were all over the country* from the word it modifies, *towns*. Choice **E** causes similar problems by separating the verb *were* from *all over the country*. Choice **D** confuses the words so much, the sentence is no longer complete. Choice **B**, however, makes it clear that the small towns were *throughout the country*. This is the answer you are looking for.

6. **A**

When making a comparison, the items being compared must be parallel. In this sentence, the author compares *leading with his left hand* to *leading with his right*. The items compared are in the same form, which means choice **A** is the answer; the sentence contains no overt errors. Choices **B** and **C** are similar in that the first half of the comparison starts out with *leading with his left hand*. Notice that in both cases, the second item being compared does not include the verb *leading*, or any verb at all. The comparisons are not parallel. Choices **D** and **E** on the surface look okay because they both use the verb *leading* in both halves of the comparison. However, things become garbled because in both cases, the actual comparison—*as skillful as*—is inserted in the middle of the comparison instead of at the beginning.

7.   E

This sentence opens awkwardly. The modifying phrase, *which was cold*, is excessively wordy, and slows down our ability to understand what happened *on the river*. You are looking for an answer choice that simplifies and clarifies the sentence. Choice **A** therefore is incorrect. Choice **B** exacerbates the wordiness by inserting the phrase *which being cold*. Choices **C** and **D** similarly complicate the sentence. Choice **E**, however, simplifies the sentence in a concise fashion by placing the adjective *cold* right before *weather*.

8.   A

You should immediately notice the semicolon separating the two halves of this sentence. Remember that a semicolon should be used to separate two complete clauses. The first half of the sentence is *an education is a difficult thing to buy*. This is a complete sentence, expressing a complete thought. The second half of the sentence is *only through hard work can one really learn*. This is also a complete sentence, capable of standing on its own. Both halves of the sentence are complete and correctly combined by a semicolon; this sentence contains no grammatical errors, so the correct answer is choice **A**. Choices **B** and **C** are faulty because they start the second halves of their respective sentences with the conjunction *but*; it is impossible to start a complete sentence with the word *but*. Choice **D** makes the second half of the sentence awkward by using the passive voice; *only hard work lets one learn*. Choice **E** is clumsy.

9.   C

You should immediately pick up on the fact that the underlined portion contains two pronouns, and check for errors in pronoun use. Remember that a pronoun must refer back clearly to one noun and agree with that noun in number. This sentence repeats the pronoun *they*. But it is unclear who *they* are. Does *they* refer to *employees* or to *someone*? To clarify this problem, *they* must be used to refer to only one very obvious noun. Choice **A** therefore cannot be the correct answer. Choice **E** does not solve the problem because it continues to use the pronoun *they* and *their* in an unclear fashion. Choice **B** inserts the phrase *the reason being*, which causes awkwardness. Choice **D** moves the verb *appreciated* to the end of the sentence and uses the undesirable passive voice. Choice **C** clears up all the confusion by replacing one of the pronouns with the word *someone*.

Using the correction supplied in choice **C**, you can easily understand that the *employees* might have been promoted because *someone liked the way* that the *employees worked hard.*

SET 3: PARAGRAPH IMPROVEMENT

(1) Ludwig van Beethoven, one of the world's most famous composers, was born in Bonn in 1770. (2) Ludwig's father encouraged his son to play the piano, hoping that the boy would become a child prodigy. (3) Ludwig gave his first public performance when he was eight years old. (4) Employed as a musician in the Bonn court orchestra since 1787, Beethoven was granted a paid leave of absence in 1789 to travel to Vienna and study with Mozart. (5) He was compelled to return to Bonn so that he could look after his family after the death of his mother.

(6) In 1792 he moved back to Vienna and took lessons from Haydn and Salieri. (7) By 1795 he had earned a name for himself as a pianist of great fantasy and verve, and he was especially renowned for his originality. (8) Beethoven was also very interested in the development of the piano. (9) He worked with piano-building firms in Austria and England and helped in the development of the modern concert piano.

(10) Around 1798 Beethoven noticed that he was beginning to lose his hearing. (11) He withdrew from the public eye and limited his social contact to a few trusted friends. (12) People who understood his frustration and were patient with his disability. (13) The final years of his life were dominated by severe illness and by his responsibilities to his family. (14) He died in 1827, and some thirty thousand mourners and curious onlookers attended his funeral procession.

1. In context, what would be the best subject for a sentence to be inserted between sentences 3 and 4?

    (A) A list of Beethoven's most famous compositions
    (B) A description of Beethoven's adolescent years
    (C) A history of Beethoven's family
    (D) An analysis of Beethoven's skill as a composer
    (E) A question about Beethoven's motivations for moving to
         Vienna

2. In context, what would be the best word to insert at the beginning of sentence 5?

    (A) Undoubtedly,
    (B) Moreover,
    (C) Unfortunately,
    (D) Typically,
    (E) Surprisingly,

3. Which of the following is the best revision of sentence 7 (reproduced below)?

    > By 1795 he had earned a name for himself as a pianist of great fantasy and verve, and he was especially renowned for his originality.

    (A) By 1795 he had earned a name for himself as a pianist of
         great fantasy, verve, and, most of all, originality.
    (B) By 1795 he has earned a name for himself as a pianist of
         great fantasy and verve, and he is especially renowned
         for his originality.
    (C) By 1795 he had earned a name for himself as a pianist of
         great fantasy and verve. And, he was especially
         renowned for his originality.
    (D) By 1795 he had earned a name for himself as a pianist of
         great fantasy and verve; and was especially renowned
         for his originality.
    (E) By 1795 he had earned a name for himself as, most, of all a
         pianist of great fantasy, verve, and originality.

4. In context, what is the best way to deal with sentence 12?

    (A) Insert "Such" before "people".
    (B) Place it before sentence 11.
    (C) Connect it to sentence 11 with a semicolon.
    (D) Connect it to sentence 11 with a comma.
    (E) Leave it as it is now.

5. What description best fits the passage as a whole?

    (A) An analysis of German music
    (B) A piece written in praise of Beethoven's genius
    (C) A study of the effects of illness on productivity
    (D) A parody of Beethoven's character
    (E) A short biographical history

ANSWERS & EXPLANATIONS

1. **B**

The passage introduces Ludwig van Beethoven as the subject. In sentences 1, 2, and 3, we learn when Beethoven was born, how his father encouraged him, and when he gave his first performance. In line 4, the paragraph jumps ahead in the chronological account of Beethoven's life to tell us about his job in the Bonn court orchestra, seventeen years after he was born. What is missing is an account of Beethoven's life between the ages of eight and seventeen. In context, it would make sense for the passage to include a little bit about *Beethoven's adolescent years*, choice **B**. The passage does not list Beethoven's most famous compositions, choice **A**; chronologically speaking, Beethoven has not yet started to write his most famous pieces. *A history of Beethoven's family*, choice **C**, might make sense earlier in the paragraph but not in between lines 3 and 4. Choice **D**, *an analysis of Beethoven's skill as a composer*, is also beyond the scope of the first paragraph, which tells you about the early part of Beethoven's life. Beethoven does not move to Vienna in the context of the passage until the end of sentence 4; it makes no sense to question his *motivations for moving to Vienna*, choice **E**, so early in the first paragraph.

2. **C**

In sentence 4, you learn that Beethoven was given money to leave Bonn to study with Mozart. In sentence 5, you are told that Beethoven was *compelled* to come home again to care for his mother. The passage has set up a contrast in behavior; on the one hand, Beethoven leaves home but then sadly returns. You know that this is an unfortunate circumstance because the passage uses the words *compelled to return*, which essentially mean *forced to return*. You need a connecting word that highlights this reverse in behavior. Choice **C**, *unfortunately*, correctly captures the sense that Beethoven has changed his mind. We have no idea if this kind of behavior is *typical*, choice **D**, or *surprising*, choice **E**, for Beethoven, as nothing in the passage so far would indicate that either word makes sense. *Moreover*, choice **B**, does not express that Beethoven was *compelled* to return home. *Undoubtedly*, choice **A**, also does not address the unfortunate turn of events for Beethoven's education.

3.   **A**

When items are listed in a sentence, they need to be placed in parallel form. Sentence 7 lists three items: *great fantasy, verve,* and *originality*. Notice, however, that the third item in the list, *originality,* is saddled with a clause; *he was especially renowned*. The other two items in the list, *great fantasy* and *verve,* are not accompanied by this extraneous information. In order for this sentence to read correctly, you need to find a solution that will place all three items in the same form. Choices **B**, **C**, and **D** do not fix the problem. Choice **B** is wrong because it does not even attempt to fix the problem. Choice **C** puts the third item in the list into a second sentence, but *and, he was especially renowned for his originality* is an incomplete sentence and causes a whole new set of problems. Choice **D** attempts to separate the third item in the list from the rest of the sentence with a semicolon, but this still does not put all the items in the list in parallel form. Choice **E** might tempt you, which ends with the list *great fantasy, verve, and originality*. However, notice that the earlier part of choice E contains this clumsy wording, *as, most, of all*. It is incorrect to separate the comparative phrase *most of all* by commas, making choice **E** grammatically incorrect. Only choice **A** solves the problem. The sentence in choice **A** ends as follows: . . . *great fantasy, verve, and, most of all, originality*. Now the three items—*fantasy, verve,* and *originality*—are all listed as nouns; in other words, they are listed in parallel form.

4.   **D**

Notice that sentence 12 is a fragment; it does not express a complete thought. If you insert "Such" before "people," choice **A**, you would have the following: *Such people who understood his frustration and were patient with his disability*. This still does not make sentence 12 complete. Moving sentence 12 around, choice **B**, or leaving it as it is, choice **E**, also does not fix the inherent problem that sentence 12 is a fragment. You can only connect two sentences together with a semicolon, choice **C**, if both sentences are complete sentences in the first place. As you know, sentence 12 is a fragment, and therefore using a semicolon does not help. However, if you connect sentence 12 to sentence 11 via a comma, you would have the following result: *He withdrew from the public eye and limited his social contact to a few trusted friends, people who understood his frustration and were patient with his disability.* In this case, the clause *people who . . . disability* would modify *a few trusted friends*, creating one longer but complete sentence. Only choice **D** provides you with a grammatically correct way to deal with sentence 12.

5.   **E**

The passage as a whole gives you a quick account of Beethoven, a formidable German composer. You need to find the answer choice that best restates this. Choices **A** and **C** are beyond the scope of this passage. Choice **A** is wrong because you are not presented with an analysis of all German music; the discussion is limited to Beethoven. Choice **C** is wrong because the passage isn't just about illness, although Beethoven does get sick toward the end of the passage. Choices **B** and **D** may be tempting if you missed the tone of the passage. On the whole, there is very little to suggest that the author is really *praising* Beethoven, **B**, or making fun of him, **D**. The author uses very neutral words to recount Beethoven's life, occasionally pointing out how *other* people felt about the composer but rarely offering a personal assessment. Only **E** sums up the author's intention, which is to provide a *short biographical history.*

SET 4: SENTENCE ERROR ID

1. Because the <u>doctor's</u> approach to treating infection <u>differed from</u>
               A   B

    his <u>peers</u>, he was often <u>thought of</u> as being somewhat radical.
        C   D

    <u>No error</u>
      E

2. The <u>honor of</u> receiving several <u>distinguished-service</u> awards
           A   B

    <u>have</u> made the elderly man forget all about his <u>disputes with</u> his
      C   D

    neighbors. <u>No error</u>
             E

3. After <u>entering</u> the hospital, the patient looked <u>around trying</u> to
           A   B

    find a nurse <u>which</u> could tell him where <u>he should</u> wait. <u>No error</u>
              C   D   E

4. The <u>importance of</u> regular visits to the doctor <u>are</u> not to be
           A   B

    underestimated <u>in</u> maintenance of a healthy <u>lifestyle</u>. <u>No error</u>
                 C   D   E

5. <u>That</u> the history professor was able to lecture so eruditely
      A

    <u>on a period</u> <u>with which he</u> himself was unfamiliar <u>was</u> surprising
       B   C   D

    to his peers. <u>No error</u>
               E

6. Of the two late arrivals, David was by far <u>the least</u>
                                            A

    <u>apprehensive about</u> meeting other people at the wedding party,
         B

    <u>since</u> he was generally comfortable <u>in groups</u>. <u>No error</u>
      C   D   E

7. <u>Regardless of</u> whether the fire <u>was set</u> on purpose or
     A   B
   <u>unintentional</u>, the person <u>responsible</u> must be punished to the
        C   D
   full extent of the law. <u>No error</u>
                                E

8. If one wishes to save money, <u>you</u> should not <u>give in to</u> the
                                  A   B
   temptation of schemes <u>designed</u> to make money <u>quickly</u>.
                           C   D
   <u>No error</u>
      E

9. It is important <u>to graduate</u> from high school, because there
                      A
   <u>are hardly no</u> jobs <u>available</u> for <u>those</u> who do not finish. <u>No error</u>
        B   C   D   E

10. At the board meeting, the owner <u>of</u> the corporation disclosed
                                       A
    that a large proportion of <u>their</u> profits had come from activities
                                 B
    <u>not approved</u> by <u>its</u> stockholders. <u>No error</u>
        C   D   E

ANSWERS & EXPLANATIONS

1.　C

The subject *approach* is correctly modified by the possessive word *doctor's*, choice **A**. The sentence will not just tell you about an *approach*, but specifically about the *doctor's approach*. The verb *differed from*, choice **B**, correctly agrees with the subject of the sentence, *approach*. The preposition *from* in *differed from*, choice **B**, is idiomatic and is without error. Choice **C**, *his peers*, attempts to let us know what the *doctor's approach . . . differed from*. However, the word *peers* has not been converted to a possessive. To be correct, the aword *peers'* should be used. Choice **C** contains an error and therefore is the correct answer to this question.

2.　C

Choice **A**, *honor of*, contains the subject of the sentence, followed by a preposition. There is no error here. The hyphenated modifier *distinguished-service*, choice **B**, correctly modifies the plural noun *awards*. However, the verb *have*, choice **C**, is intended to refer back to the subject of the sentence, which is the noun *honor*. Notice, however, that while the subject *honor* is singular, the verb *have* is plural. Choice **C** contains an error and therefore is the correct answer to this question. You may have thought that choice **C** was without error and that the verb *have* was supposed to agree with the plural noun *awards*. Note, however, that *awards* is the object of a prepositional phrase, *of receiving several distinguished-service awards.* This long phrase merely tells you what kind of *honor* the author is about to discuss; the phrase alone is not the subject. Finally, the idiomatic expression *disputes with*, choice **D**, is without error.

3.   **C**

The verb *entering*, **A**, is correct; there is no error here. Reading further, you learn that the patient looked *around trying*, choice **B**, to find someone. This is an idiomatic expression and is without error. Who was the patient trying to find? A *nurse.* Unfortunately, the noun *nurse* is modified by the demonstrative pronoun *which*, choice **C**, but a *nurse* is a person and must be modified by the pronoun *who.* Choice **C** contains an error and is the correct answer to the question. The pronoun *he*, choice **D**, correctly refers back to the noun *patient*, and the verb *should* agrees in number with this pronoun.

4.   **B**

The subject of this sentence is the noun *importance*, choice **A**, which is followed by the preposition *of*, signaling that the word *importance* is about to be modified by a prepositional phrase. There is no error here. The verb *are*, choice **B**, is supposed to agree with the subject of the sentence, *importance.* However, note that while the subject, *importance*, is singular, the verb, *are*, is plural. Recall that a verb must always agree with its subject. Choice **B** contains an error and is the correct answer to this question. The preposition *in*, choice **C**, introduces the modifying phrase *in maintenance of a healthy lifestyle* and is used correctly. The noun *lifestyle*, choice **D**, is the object of the prepositional phrase *of a healthy lifestyle* and is without error.

5.   **E**

The sentence may sound a little clumsy to you, but it doesn't contain any grammatical errors. The main subject of the sentence is the pronoun *that*, **A**, followed by the entire clause it modifies; *the history teacher was able to lecture so eruditely on a period with which he himself was unfamil-*

iar. The verb *was*, choice **D**, is the main verb of the sentence. Both the subject and the verb agree with each other and contain no grammatical errors. The preposition *on*, choice **B**, is part of the idiomatic expression *to lecture . . . on*, and it provides us with information about the professor's lecture. The prepositional phrase *with which he*, choice **C**, tells us more about the period; it was a period *with which* the professor was *unfamiliar*. There are no errors in this sentence, which means the correct answer is choice **E**.

6.   **A**

You are told that there are only two late arrivals—David and one other person. To be correct, the comparative phrase *the least*, choice **A**, would need to be replaced by the word *less*. The comparative term *the least* would only be correct if the author were comparing at least three people. Choice **A** has an error and is the correct answer to this question. The idiomatic expression *apprehensive about*, choice **B**, is used correctly. The adverb *since*, choice **C**, introduces the clause *since he was generally comfortable* and is used without error. The modifying phrase *in groups*, choice **D**, tells you where David was generally *comfortable*.

7.   **C**

The idiomatic expression *regardless of*, choice **A**, is used correctly at the start of this sentence. The verb *was set*, choice **B**, agrees with its modifying subject, *fire*. The author then goes on to tell you how the fire might have been *set—on purpose or unintentional*. Remember, however, that it is necessary to modify all verbs using adverbs. The word *unintentional*, choice **C**, is an adjective and therefore is used incorrectly. To fix this problem, you would need to replace the adjective *unintentional* with the adverb *unintentionally*. Hence, the answer to this question is choice **C**. The adjective *responsible*, choice **D**, correctly modifies the noun *person* and is used without error.

8.   **A**

The sentence begins with the phrase *if one wishes*. However, in the second half of the sentence, the pronoun *one* is replaced with the pronoun *you*, choice **A**. It is necessary to be consistent when using *one* or *you*; it is incorrect to use both within the same sentence. Since choice **A** contains an error, it is the correct answer to this question. The idiomatic phrase *give in to*, choice **B**, is used without error. The verb *designed*, choice **C**, agrees with the noun *temptation*. The adverb *quickly*, choice **D**, tells us in what manner you might be tempted *to make money*.

9.   B

The infinitive form of the verb *to graduate*, choice **A**, is used without error. However, choice **B**, *are hardly no*, contains a double negative. Remember, words like *hardly*, *scarcely*, and *never* are negative words; placing them alongside another negative word, like *no*, creates a double negative. For the sentence to be without errors, the author would need to remove the word *no* from choice **B** and replace it with the word *any*. As it stands, choice **B** contains an error and is the correct answer to this question. The adjective *available*, choice **C**, correctly modifies the word *jobs*. The pronoun *those*, choice **D**, is in the correct form to follow the preposition *for*.

10.   B

The preposition *of*, choice **A**, introduces the prepositional phrase *of the corporation*, correctly modifying the noun *owner*. The pronoun *their*, choice **B**, is supposed to tell you whose *profits had come from activities not approved by its stockholders*. To check and see if this form of the pronoun is correct, you need to determine which noun it refers to; in this case, the *profits* belong to the *owner of the corporation*. Note that the word *owner* is singular, while the pronoun *their* is plural. However, a pronoun must always agree in number with the noun it is referring to; choice **B** contains an error and is the correct answer to this question. To read correctly, you would need to replace the pronoun *their* with either *he* or *she*. The verb *not approved*, choice **C**, agrees with the noun it modifies, *activities*. The pronoun *its*, choice **D**, refers back to the word *corporation*; in other words, the corporation's *stockholders* had *not approved* of the activities that yielded so much *profit*.

SET 5: SENTENCE IMPROVEMENT

1. Shakespeare wrote <u>plays and they reflect</u> both the depth of human emotion and the complexity of human society.

   (A) plays and they reflect
   (B) plays that reflect
   (C) plays, who reflect
   (D) plays, being that they reflect
   (E) plays, being a reflection of

2. Because the student got no sleep the night before, <u>causing him to fall</u> asleep during the last section of the examination.

   (A) causing him to fall
   (B) and so he fell
   (C) he fell
   (D) and he fell
   (E) so falling

3. <u>Having a particularly good view of the ocean, the tourists chose the hotel</u> to be their home base for the duration of their holiday.

   (A) Having a particularly good view of the ocean, the tourists chose the hotel
   (B) Having a particularly good view of the ocean, the hotel was chosen by the tourists
   (C) Because its view of the ocean was particularly good, the tourists chose the hotel
   (D) The hotel's particularly good view of the ocean led to its choice by the tourists
   (E) The tourists chose the hotel, because it had a particularly good view of the ocean

4. The idea that the world will become a battleground for gods and giants is at the heart of Norse mythology.

    (A) The idea that the world will become a battleground for gods and giants is at the heart of Norse mythology.
    (B) The idea that the world will become a battleground for gods and giants in Norse mythology is at its heart.
    (C) The world will become a battleground for gods and giants is an idea at the heart of Norse mythology.
    (D) The idea at the heart of Norse mythology, the world will become a battle ground for gods and giants.
    (E) In Norse mythology the idea in their hearts is that the world will become a battleground for gods and giants.

5. The excellent atmospheric conditions allowed the astronomer to see the stars and he could even discern the shapes of the craters on the moon.

    (A) he could even discern
    (B) even discerning
    (C) so he could even discern
    (D) even a discernment of
    (E) even to discern

6. The left-handed can opener was a brilliant invention; the popularization of electric can openers made them obsolete, however.

    (A) invention; the popularization of electric can openers made it obsolete, however.
    (B) invention; but the popularization of the electric can opener made it obsolete.
    (C) invention, and the popularization of the electric can opener made it obsolete.
    (D) invention, however the popularization of the electric can opener made it obsolete.
    (E) invention, however obsolete it was made by the invention of the electric can opener.

7. For many academics, <u>having the liberty to teach what they want is more important</u> than having a good salary.

    (A) having the liberty to teach what they want is more important

    (B) the liberty of teaching what they want is more important

    (C) there is more importance in being free to teach what they want

    (D) to have the liberty to teach what they want is more important

    (E) liberty to teach what they want has more importance

8. Many recent <u>films are based around natural disasters, named in order to evoke fear in audiences.</u>

    (A) films are based around natural disasters, named in order to evoke fear in audiences.

    (B) films, based around natural disasters, are named in order to evoke fear in audiences.

    (C) films are named in order to evoke fear in audiences, based on natural disasters.

    (D) films having their names based on natural disasters are meant to evoke fear in audiences.

    (E) films based around natural disasters are named in order to evoke fear in audiences.

9. <u>The conscientious driver pulled out of the driveway looking in both directions.</u>

    (A) The conscientious driver pulled out of the driveway looking in both directions.

    (B) The conscientious driver pulled out of the driveway and looking in both directions.

    (C) Pulling out of the driveway and looking in both directions was the conscientious driver.

    (D) Looking in both directions, the conscientious driver pulled out of the driveway.

    (E) The driver looking in both directions was conscientious pulling out of the driveway.

10. <u>Considering his tremendous donations to charity</u>, the millionaire's decision to close the school seems out of character.

   (A) Considering his tremendous donations to charity

   (B) In light of his tremendous donations to charity

   (C) His tremendous donations to charity being considered

   (D) With his tremendous donations to charity being taken into consideration

   (E) His tremendous donations to charity are what make

ANSWERS & EXPLANATIONS

1. **B**

You should note right away that the underlined portion of this sentence includes the conjunction *and.* Remember, when combining two clauses in a sentence with a conjunction, one of the clauses needs to be dependent on the other. The two must also be combined with a comma. However, take a look at the first clause: *Shakespeare wrote plays.* This is a complete sentence. Now look at the second clause: *they reflect both the depth of human emotion and the complexity of human society.* This is also a complete sentence; the original sentence violates the rule of usage where conjunctions are concerned, and choice **A** is incorrect. Choice **B** immediately fixes the problem by replacing *and they* with the demonstrative pronoun *that.* The second half of the sentence, *that reflect . . . human society* now modifies *play*, telling us exactly what Shakespeare wrote. Choice **C** contains the pronoun *who*, but *who* can only refer to a person and therefore cannot refer to the noun *plays.* Choices **D** and **E** are both unnecessarily wordy and clumsy; you are looking for an answer that simplifies and corrects the problem.

2. **C**

The clause *because the student got no sleep the night before* is dependent and must be followed by a complete sentence. Read *causing him to fall asleep during the last section of the examination* out loud and you realize pretty quickly that the second half of the sentence is a fragment. To fix this error, you need to replace *causing him to fall* with something that makes the second half of the sentence an independent clause. Choice **A** cannot be the correct answer. Choices **B** and **D** both begin with the conjunction *and* but don't continue on in complete sentences. Choice **E** is a problem because it completely removes the subject, *he*, from the sentence. Choice **C**, however, replaces *causing him to fall* with *he fell*. The second half of the sentence now reads *he fell asleep during the last section of the examination*. This expresses a clear thought.

3. **C**

The modifying clause *having a particularly good view of the ocean* is intended to modify the noun *hotel*. In other words, the sentence tells you that the *hotel* has a *good view of the ocean*. Because *the tourists* immediately follows the modifying phrase, however, the sentence implies that the tourists have a good view of the ocean, not the hotel. To fix this problem, find an answer choice that makes it clear *what* has a good view of the ocean. Choice **B** may be tempting because *the hotel* comes directly after the modifying phrase. Note, however, that the rest of the sentence is passive and you should avoid passive sentence constructions. There must be a better answer. Choice **E** creates a new problem; according to this wording, *the view of the ocean* will become the home base, which makes no sense. Logically, you know that the *hotel* will become the *home base*. Choice **D** is clunky and wordy. Now try to read the correction suggested by choice **C**. *Because its view of the ocean was particularly good, the tourists chose the hotel to be their home base for the duration of their holiday.* The modifier and the modifying clause are placed next to each other, and the meaning of the sentence is clear.

4. **A**

The entire sentence is underlined, giving you no real clue as to where the problem might be. A quick check of the subject and the verb shows that the two agree; *idea* and *is at the heart* fit together. The modifying clause *that the world will become* is also placed correctly, giving you further information about *idea*. Choice **E** cannot be the correct answer because the pronoun *their* does not relate to any clear antecedent; whose *hearts* does *their* refer to? *The idea at the heart of Norse mythology*, choice **D**, is a fragment and lacks a verb to turn it into a clear idea. In choice **C**, the main verb, *is*, has no subject to anchor itself to. What *is an idea at the heart of Norse mythology*? The wording in choice **C** does not tell you. The possessive pronoun *its* in choice **B** is also vague. At whose *heart* is the idea that *the world will become a battleground for gods and giants*? The answer is choice **A**, as there is nothing wrong with the sentence in the first place.

5. **E**

Items, or actions in a list, must be in parallel form. The *excellent atmospheric conditions* allowed the astronomer to do two things: first—*to see the stars*—and second—*he could even discern*. Notice that the first item in the list does not use the pronoun *he*, while the second item in the list does. In order to follow the rules of correct usage, the second item in the list, which is also the underlined portion of the sentence, must be parallel to the first item in the list. Choice **A** cannot be the correct answer. Choice **E** removes the pronoun *he* and places the verb *discern* in its infinitive form; now the two items in the list are parallel. This is the correct answer to the question. Choice **C** is wrong because it continues to retain the pronoun *he*. Choice **B** places the verb *discern* in its participle form—*discerning*. This still does not put the verbs in parallel form. Similarly, choice **D** drops the pronoun *he* but puts the verb *discern* into its noun form, *discernment*. This also fails to place the listed items in parallel form.

6. **A**

Be alerted by the semicolon separating the two clauses in this sentence. Remember, a semicolon can only be used if the two halves of a sentence are independent and able to stand on their own. The first half of the sentence is *the left-handed can opener was a brilliant invention*; this is a complete sentence. The second half reads *the popularization of electric can openers made it obsolete, however*. This is also an independent clause. The word *however* does dangle on the end, but it does not violate any major rule of correct English usage. There is no error in this sentence, and choice **A** is the correct answer. Choice **B** is wrong because it includes the word *but*, which makes the second sentence a dependent clause. Recall that in order to use a semicolon, the two halves of a sentence must be independent of each other. Choice **C** introduces the word *and*. However, the two halves of the sentence are intended to show some contrast; while *the left-handed can opener was a brilliant invention, electric can openers* rendered that great invention *obsolete*. The word *and* does not adequately demonstrate this contrast. Choice **D** is problematic because it is not clear what the pronoun *it* refers to; a pronoun must have one clear antecedent. Choice **E** includes the wordy and awkward phrase *however obsolete it was*.

7.　**A**

The modifying phrase *having the liberty to teach what they want is more important* is underlined, and refers back to the noun, *academics*. You are told that many academics value freedom in teaching more than a salary. Two items are being compared here. The sentence compares *having the liberty to teach* to *having a good salary*. Remember, when two items are being compared, they must be in parallel form. The original wording of the sentence, choice **A**, is the correct answer because the compared items are expressed in the same format. Choices **E** and **C** have eliminated the verb *having*; the items being compared are not in parallel form. Choice **D** retains the verb *to have*, but does not retain the correct form of the verb, which is *having*. Choice **B** compares *having a good salary* to *the liberty of teaching*, which again does not keep the compared items in a parallel format.

8.　**B**

The comma in the underlined portion of the sentence should alert you. The second half of the sentence, *named in order to evoke fear in audiences*, is a fragment. Choice **A** is not the correct answer; you need to find some answer choice that eliminates the fragmentary nature of this sentence. Choice **B** adds a comma between *films* and *based* and the verb *are* before *named*. This causes the phrase *based around natural disasters* to modify *films* and makes *are named* the main verb of the sentence; the entire sentence is now complete. Choice **C** puts the modifying phrase *based on natural disasters* directly after *audiences*, which makes it sound as though the *audiences* are based on *natural disasters*; this isn't logical. Excessive wordiness and awkwardness plague choice **D**. Choice **E** may be tempting because it resembles choice **B** on the surface, but the lack of commas makes it unclear if the verb *are* is supposed to go with *disasters* or with *films*.

9.　**D**

The modifier *looking in both directions* comes directly after the word *driveway*. As the sentence reads originally, it appears that the *driveway* is looking in both directions. Clearly this is not logical; it is the *driver* that is looking *in both directions*. Choice **A** cannot be the correct answer. You need to find an answer choice that places the modifier in the right place. Unfortunately, the verb *looking* in choice **B** is in the wrong form; it sounds clunky. Choice **C** is awkward; you are forced to wait until the end of the sentence to find out the subject. Choice **E** is also awkward; it moves the adjective *conscientious* far away from the noun *driver*. The correction suggested by choice **D** solves the original problem; it clearly demonstrates that *the conscientious driver* looked in both directions and proceeded to pull out of the driveway.

10. **B**

The verb, *considering*, is unclear here because it could imply two meanings. On the one hand, perhaps the millionaire *is considering his tremendous donations to charity*. On the other hand, perhaps you the reader are meant to consider the millionaire's *tremendous donations to charity*. The only way to ensure that this sentence is clear is to rewrite it; choice **A** cannot be the answer. Choice **D** causes similar problems; this solution sounds as though the millionaire is taking into consideration his own tremendous donations to charity. Choice **B**, however, makes the meaning of the sentence completely obvious: *The millionaire's decision to close the school seems out of character in light of*, or due to, *his tremendous donations to charity.* Choice **C** uses the clumsy passive voice, *being considered.* Choice **E** is also clumsy and awkward.

SET 6: PARAGRAPH IMPROVEMENT

(1) Western Europe was beginning to look like a cultural wasteland when Charlemagne became king of the Franks in 768. **(2)** Education and the arts, which flourished under the rule of the Roman Empire, had been largely banished to monasteries. **(3)** Charlemagne recognized the importance of these cultural riches and took steps to restore them to their places as cornerstones of society.

(4) Charlemagne's family upbringing is probably what led him to place so much value on art and education. **(5)** Although schools had almost disappeared in the eighth century, historians believe that Charlemagne's mother, Bertrade, taught the young prince to read. **(6)** His devotion to the church, which became the great driving force of his remarkable life, would also have inclined Charlemagne to emphasize education. **(7)** Monasteries depended on young men who could read and write to copy religious texts.

(8) Perhaps the most remarkable cultural achievement of Charlemagne's reign was the standardization of Carolingian Minuscule. **(9)** A style of handwriting that resembled the lowercase letters used for written English and many other languages today. **(10)** In previous centuries, styles of handwriting had become so diverse that scribes would often make mistakes while copying books by hand. **(11)** As a consequence, the meaning of important texts would often be distorted or obscured. **(12)** Charlemagne may have appreciated arts and education, but he did not turn his nose up at life's simple pleasures. **(13)** He took particular satisfaction from athletic pursuits such as hunting, riding, and swimming. **(14)** Such activities may have been more than pastimes, however. **(15)** As the commander of a powerful army, the king would often lead his troops into battle, it was important that he keep himself in prime physical condition.

1.   In context, what is the most logical word to insert at the beginning of
     sentence 3?

     (A) Moreover,
     (B) Unnecessarily,
     (C) Undoubtedly,
     (D) Unfortunately,
     (E) However,

2.   The desired effect of the second paragraph is to

     (A) summarize two contrasting opinions
     (B) offer possible explanations for the events described
          elsewhere in the passage
     (C) emphasize the importance of the thesis
     (D) incite an emotional reaction from the reader
     (E) argue the points made in the first paragraph from a
          different perspective

3.   In context, what is the most effective way to deal with sentence 9?

     (A) Join it to sentence 8 with a comma.
     (B) Insert "Which was" before "a style".
     (C) Place it after sentence 10.
     (D) Move "that resembled" to the beginning of the sentence.
     (E) Leave it as it is now.

4.   Which of the following subjects would be most appropriate for a
     sentence to insert at the end of the third paragraph?

     (A) The importance of books in education
     (B) The relationship between physical exercise and intelligence
     (C) Charlemagne's devotion to Christianity
     (D) Charlemagne's tastes in literature
     (E) Charlemagne's military prowess

5.   What change should be made to correct sentence 15?

     (A) Change "as" to "he was".
     (B) Change the first comma to a semicolon.
     (C) Change the second comma to a semicolon
     (D) Change "condition" to "shape".
     (E) Place it before sentence 14.

ANSWERS & EXPLANATIONS

1.   E

In sentence 2, you are told that *education and the arts . . . had been largely banished to monasteries.* In other words, *education and the arts* stopped being a part of mainstream society. In sentence 3, you learn that Charlemagne *took steps to restore them to their places as cornerstones of society*; Charlemagne tried to bring *education and the arts* back into the world. The passage has set up a contrast between these two sentences. The word *however,* choice **E**, emphasizes this contrast. *Moreover,* choice **A**, indicates that the passage is about to continue a point made in the previous sentence. But you already know that the passage is setting up a contrast between sentences 2 and 3. *Moreover* would only logically make sense if the content of sentence 3 strengthened a point made in sentence 2, which it does not. *Unnecessarily,* choice **B**, is problematic because it runs counter to the tone of the passage. The passage praises Charlemagne, citing his most remarkable *achievement,* sentence 8. The word *unnecessarily* would negate the passage's praise of Charlemagne and therefore does not logically fit in the sentence. The same holds true for *unfortunately,* choice **D**. The passage praises Charlemagne for restoring arts back to the world; there is nothing unfortunate about this act. Finally, *undoubtedly,* choice **C**, also does not logically address the contrast set up between sentences 2 and 3.

2.   B

In the first paragraph of the passage, you are told that Charlemagne *took steps to restore* the arts and education *to their places as cornerstones of society.* He did this even though *Western Europe was beginning to look like a cultural wasteland.* You are told that this remarkable king, Charlemagne, did something that was highly unusual for his time. The second paragraph opens with the sentence *Charlemagne's family upbringing is probably what led him to place so much value on art and education.* The passage is telling you *why* Charlemagne probably took steps to restore the arts and education to mainstream society. Another way of putting this is that the second paragraph offers *possible explanations for the events described elsewhere in the passage,* choice **B**. Choice **A** is wrong because the passage does not contrast the opinions of the first paragraph with opinions in the second paragraph; the second paragraph offers an *explanation*. While it is true that the passage finds Charlemagne's accomplishments important, the second paragraph does not *emphasize the importance of Charlemagne's decisions*, choice **C**; the second paragraph tries to explain them. Choice **D** is completely beyond the intended scope of the passage; this is a fairly reasoned, intelligent passage, not something that attempts to *incite an emotional reaction*. Finally, the second paragraph helps to explain the information contained in the first paragraph; the passage is not trying to *argue the points made in the first paragraph*, choice **E**.

3.   **A**

Sentence 9 is a fragment, or an incomplete sentence. You must make this a complete sentence. The best way to do this would be to replace the period from the previous sentence with a comma and join sentences 8 and 9 together. This is precisely the remedy suggested by choice **A**. None of the other answer choices provide you with a correct way to turn sentence 9 into a complete sentence. If you follow the advice in choice **B**, you would have the following: *Which was a style of handwriting that resembled the lowercase letters used for written English and many other languages today.* This is still an incomplete sentence. Moving sentence 9 after sentence 10, choice **C**, still leaves sentence 9 as a fragment; this move would also mess up the logical flow of the passage, as the information contained in sentence 9 is intended to add to the information relayed in sentence 8. If you follow the advice of choice **D**, you would end up with the following: *that resembled a style of handwriting that resembled the lowercase letters used for written English and many other languages today.* However, this is still not a complete sentence. Finally, if you *leave* line 9 *as it is now*, choice **E**, you would still not have turned sentence 9 into a complete sentence; this can hardly be considered an *effective* solution to the problem.

4.   **A**

The third paragraph discusses how Charlemagne standardized a style of handwriting known as *Carolingian Minuscule*. The passage then goes on to tell you books were copied by hand using Carolingian Miniscule, and that due to previous nonstandardization, *the meaning of important texts was often obscured*. A logical continuation of this paragraph would have been for the passage to go on more about books and their general impor-tance, choice **A**. *Physical exercise and intelligence*, choice **B**, does not fit the parameters of paragraph 3, which focuses on handwriting and books. The same is true of choice **E**; we learn a little bit about *Charlemagne's mil-itary prowess*, but this information comes in paragraph 4 and does not fit the context of paragraph 3. Similarly, paragraph 2 mentions *Charle-magne's devotion to Christianity*, choice **C**, and his interest in reading, if not literature, choice **D**; it might be appropriate to mention these points in paragraph 2, but not in paragraph 3, which focuses specifically on texts and book copying.

5.   **C**

Sentence 15 reads as follows: *As the commander of a powerful army, the king would often lead his troops into battle, it was important that he keep himself in prime physical condition.* Notice that this is a run-on sentence; the first half, *As the . . . into battle* is a complete sentence. The second half, *it was . . . physical condition*, is also a complete sentence. In order to combine two complete sentences together, one of the sentences must be made into a subordinate clause, or a semicolon must join together both sentences. An answer choice that provides just such a solution must be found. Specifically, the correct answer choice will focus in on the area around the comma separating *into battle* from *it was*. Choice **A**, changing *as* to *he was*, keeps both halves of sentence 15 as complete sentences, and does not fix the problem. The same is also true of choice **E**; placing sentence 15 before sentence 14 does not change the fact that sentence 15 would still be a run-on sentence. Replacing the word *condition* with the word *shape*, choice **D**, also does not fix sentence 15's inherent problems. If you changed the *first comma to a semicolon*, choice **B**, you would have the following: *As the commander of a powerful army; the king would often lead his troops into battle, it was important that he keep himself in prime physical condition.* This is still a run-on sentence. Only choice **C**, changing *the second comma to a semicolon*, actually fixes the problem.

ABOUT THE AUTHOR

Doug Tarnopol brings a unique mix of talents and experience to SparkNotes and the New SAT *Power Tactics* series. He has taught and tutored students of all backgrounds and advised both students and parents in preparing for the SAT. Doug graduated magna cum laude from Cornell University in 1992, earning a B.A. in History. He continued his work in the history and sociology of science at the University of Pennsylvania, receiving an M.A. in 1996.

While in graduate school, Doug began teaching SAT test-prep classes. After completing his graduate work, Doug moved to New York City and continued working in test prep, adding PSAT, SCI HI, SAT II: Writing, SAT I: Math, GMAT, and other courses to his repertoire. In 1999, Doug became a curriculum developer, designing instructional material for state proficiency exams.

Doug also writes fiction and poetry. He is an avid drummer, biker, and reader. He currently lives in Metuchen, New Jersey.

SPARKNOTES
Power Tactics for the New SAT

The Critical Reading Section

Reading Passages
Sentence Completions

The Math Section

Algebra
Data Analysis, Statistics & Probability
Geometry
Numbers & Operations

The Writing Section

The Essay
Multiple-Choice Questions: Identifying Sentence Errors,
Improving Sentences, Improving Paragraphs

The New SAT

Test-Taking Strategies
Vocabulary Builder

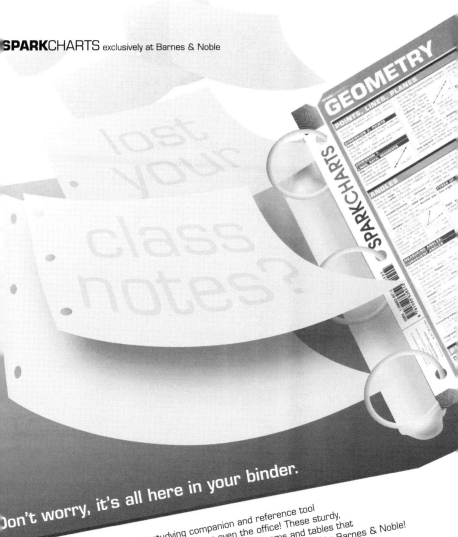

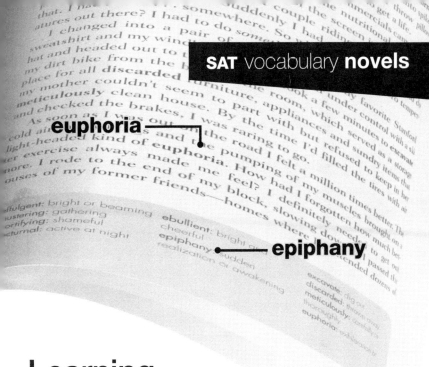

SAT vocabulary **novels**

euphoria

epiphany

Learning
—without even realizing it!

Need to study for the SATs, but would rather read a good book? Now SparkNotes®
lets you do both. Our **SAT Vocabulary Novels** are compelling full-length novels
wtih edgy and mature themes that you'll like (honest). Each book highlights more
than 1,000 vocabulary words you'll find on the SAT. Brief definitions appear at the
bottom of the page, so you can sit back, read a good book, and get some serious
studying done—all at the same time!

excerpts and more at www.sparknotes.com/**buy/satfiction/**

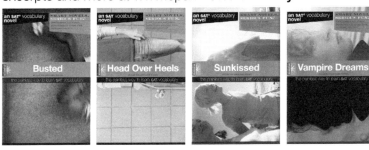